Controversial Histories – Current Views on the Crusades

Engaging the Crusades is a series of volumes which offer windows into a newly-emerging field of historical study: the memory and legacy of the Crusades. Together these volumes examine the reasons behind the enduring resonance of the Crusades and present the memory of crusading in the modern period as a productive, exciting and much needed area of investigation.

Controversial Histories assembles current international views on the Crusades from across Europe, Russia, Turkey, the USA and the Near and Middle East. Historians from the related countries present short narratives that deal with two questions: *What were the Crusades?* and *What do they mean to "us" today?* Narratives are from one of possible several "typical" points of view of the related country and present an international comparison of the dominant image of each respective historical culture and cultures of remembrance. Bringing together 'victim perspectives' and 'perpetrator perspectives', 'key players' and 'minor players', they reveal both shared and conflicting memories of different groups. The narratives are framed by an introduction about the historical and political significance of the Crusades, and the question of history education in a globalized world with contradicting narratives is discussed, along with guidelines on how to use the book for teaching at university level.

Offering extensive material and presenting a profile of international, academic opinions on the Crusades, *Controversial Histories* is the ideal resource for students and educators of Crusades history in a global context as well as military history and the history of memory.

Felix Hinz is Professor of Politics and History and their Didactics at the University of Education in Freiburg, Germany.

Johannes Meyer-Hamme is Professor of Theory and Didactics of History at the University of Paderborn, Germany.

ENGAGING THE CRUSADES

THE MEMORY AND LEGACY OF THE CRUSADES

SERIES EDITORS

JONATHAN PHILLIPS AND MIKE HORSWELL

Engaging the Crusades

The Memory and Legacy of Crusading

Series Editors: Jonathan Phillips and Mike Horswell, Royal Holloway, University of London, UK.

Engaging the Crusades is a series of volumes which offer initial windows into the ways in which the Crusades have been used in the last two centuries; demonstrating that the memory of the Crusades is an important and emerging subject. Together these studies suggest that the memory of the Crusades, in the modern period, is a productive, exciting and much needed area of investigation.

In this series:

Perceptions of the Crusades from the Nineteenth to the Twenty-First Century
Engaging the Crusades, Volume One
Edited by Jonathan Phillips and Mike Horswell

The Crusades in the Modern World
Engaging the Crusades, Volume Two
Edited by Mike Horswell and Akil N. Awan

Controversial Histories – Current Views on the Crusades
Engaging the Crusades, Volume Three
Edited by Felix Hinz and Johannes Meyer-Hamme

For more information about this series, please visit: https://www.routledge.com/Engaging-the-Crusades/book-series/ETC

Controversial Histories – Current Views on the Crusades

Engaging the Crusades, Volume Three

Edited by
Felix Hinz and
Johannes Meyer-Hamme

LONDON AND NEW YORK

First published 2021
by Routledge
2 Park Square, Milton Park, Abingdon, Oxon OX14 4RN

and by Routledge
52 Vanderbilt Avenue, New York, NY 10017

Routledge is an imprint of the Taylor & Francis Group, an informa business

British Library Cataloguing-in-Publication Data
A catalogue record for this book is available from the British Library

Library of Congress Cataloging-in-Publication Data
A catalog record has been requested for this book

ISBN: 978-0-367-14877-5 (hbk)
ISBN: 978-0-367-51127-2 (pbk)
ISBN: 978-0-429-05372-6 (ebk)

Typeset in Times New Roman
by codeMantra

Contents

List of figures xi
List of maps xii
List of tables xiii
List of contributors xiv

1 **Introduction** 1
FELIX HINZ AND JOHANNES MEYER-HAMME

2 **Experts write about historical cultures – theoretical premises and methodological comments** 7
FELIX HINZ AND JOHANNES MEYER-HAMME

3 **International views on the Crusades** 21

3.1 The ambiguous memory of Norwegian crusading – a view from Norway 21
Kristin B. Aavitsland

3.2 'Frankish invasions' and 'a cosmic struggle between Islam and Christianity' – a view from Jordan 24
Mazhar Al-Zo'by

3.3 The idea of crusading is still alive in the West – a view from Russia 26
Vardan Ėrnestovič Bagdasarjan

3.4 *Still a particular interest in the former 'Outremer' – a (first) view from France* 29
Michel Balard

3.5 *The 'Island of the Knights' on the fault line to the Islamic world – a view from Malta* 33
Emanuel Buttigieg

3.6 *Crusades and maritime expansion – a view from Portugal* 36
Paula Maria de Carvalho Pinto Costa

3.7 *The Crusades confront the orthodox – a Greek Cypriot viewpoint* 39
Nicholas Coureas

3.8 *Western aggression and Greco-Latin interaction – a view from Greece* 42
Nikolaos G. Chrissis

3.9 *The former victors over the Crusades in Palestine – a view from Egypt* 45
Taef Kamal El-Azhari

3.10 *A hostile and aggressive stance of the West towards Turkey based on othering and a double standard – a view from Turkey* 47
Mehmet Ersan

3.11 *A Crusader-flag falling from the sky – a view from Denmark* 50
Iben Fonnesberg Schmidt

3.12 *Reconquista as Crusade? – a view from Spain* 53
Luis García-Guijarro Ramos

3.13 *The heirs of the first Crusader Kings – a view from Belgium* 56
Thérèse de Hemptinne

3.14 *In the light and shadow of Richard the Lionheart – a view from the United Kingdom* 59
Mike Horswell and Jonathan Phillips

3.15 *A state of continuous rape and violation – a view from Syria* 62
Mohamad Isa

3.16 *The deplorable Crusades – a view from Sweden* 64
Kurt Villads Jensen

3.17 *Neither Rome nor Baghdad: the Crusades – a view from Ireland* 67
Conor Kostick

3.18 *For too long French historians were not critical enough – a (second) view from France* 70
Guy Lobrichon

3.19 *In the frontiers of the former kingdom of Jerusalem: risk of misunderstandings – a view from Israel* 72
Sophia Menache

3.20 *Fighting at the Nile between history and fantasy – a view from the Netherlands* 75
Jaap van Moolenbroek

3.21 *The destiny of the West. America and the Crusades – a view from the USA* 78
Mark Gregory Pegg

3.22 *From Grunwald to Vienna – a view from Poland* 81
Karol Polejowski

3.23 *The Teutonic Order forgotten today – a view from Germany* 84
Malte Prietzel

3.24 *Constantinople pillaged, Venice risen and* Gerusalemme Liberata *– a view from Italy* 87
Luigi Russo

3.25 *700 years of slavery – a view from Estonia* 89
Anti Selart

3.26 *The axe of Lalli and the cap of St. Henry – a view from Finland* 91
Miikka Tamminen

3.27 *The Crusaders as allies – a view from Georgia* 94
Mamuka Tsurtsumia

4 First interpretations of the case studies 98
FELIX HINZ AND JOHANNES MEYER-HAMME

5 Historical education under the conditions of conflicting narratives in a globalized world 119
FELIX HINZ AND JOHANNES MEYER-HAMME

6 Methodological suggestions and concrete tasks for working with this book at school and university level 129
FELIX HINZ AND JOHANNES MEYER-HAMME

7 Epilogue 132
FELIX HINZ AND JOHANNES MEYER-HAMME

Index 135

Figures

2.1 Matrix of historical thinking (Rüsen 2017, p. 43) 10

Maps

4.1 References mentioned in the contributions and resulting "narrative families" of the crusade history 105

Tables

2.1 Constructions of meaning of the Crusades (F. Hinz and J. Meyer-Hamme based on A. Körber) 13
4.1 Important dates of the Crusades mentioned in the articles 101
4.2 Myths of the Crusades mentioned in the articles 110
4.3 Monuments related to the Crusades mentioned in the articles 115

Contributors

Kristin B. Aavitsland is Professor of Medieval Studies at MF Norwegian School of Theology, Religion and Society, Centre for the Advanced Study of Religion (MF CASR), Oslo, Norway.

Mazhar Al-Zo'by is Associate Professor in Culture and Politics at the Department of International Affairs (DIA) at Qatar University, Qatar.

Vardan Ėrnestovič Bagdasarjan is Professor of History at the Moscow Region State University, Russia.

Michel Balard is Professor em. of Medieval History from the University Paris 1 Panthéon-Sorbonne, France.

Emanuel Buttigieg is Senior Lecturer in Early Modern History at the University of Malta, Malta.

Nikolaos G. Chrissis is Assistant Professor of Medieval European History at the Democritus University of Thrace, Greece.

Paula Maria de Carvalho Pinto Costa is Associate Professor for Medieval History at the University of Porto, Portugal.

Nicholas Coureas is a Senior Researcher for Medieval History at the Cyprus Research Centre, Cyprus.

Taef Kamal El-Azhari is Professor of Islamic and Middle Eastern History at the University of Helwan, Egypt.

Mehmet Ersan is Professor of Medieval History at the Ege University, Izmir, Turkey.

Iben Fonnesberg Schmidt is Professor of Medieval History at the Aalborg University, Denmark.

Luis García-Guijarro Ramos is Professor of Medieval History at the University of Zaragoza, Spain.

Thérèse de Hemptinne is Professor of Medieval History at the Ghent University, Belgium.

Mike Horswell is a visiting tutor at the Department for Continuing Education, University of Oxford, UK.

Mohamad Isa is a former history teacher from Syria, living in Germany.

Kurt Villads Jensen is Professor of Medieval History at the Stockholm University, Sweden.

Conor Kostick is historian and writer, living in Dublin, Ireland.

Guy Lobrichon is Professor em. of Medieval Culture and Religion from the University of Avignon, France.

Sophia Menache is Professor of General History at the University of Haifa, Israel.

Jaap van Moolenbroek is Associate Professor em. of Medieval History at the VU University Amsterdam, Netherlands.

Mark Gregory Pegg is Professor of Medieval History at the Washington University in St. Louis, USA.

Jonathan Phillips is Professor of History of the Crusades at Royal Holloway, University of London, UK.

Karol Polejowski is Lecturer for Medieval History at the University of Gdansk, Poland.

Malte Prietzel is historian for Medieval History, living in Hildesheim, Germany.

Luigi Russo is Associate Professor of Medieval History at the European University of Rome, Italy.

Anti Selart is Professor of Medieval History at the University of Tartu, Estonia.

Miikka Tamminen is PhD researcher of Medieval History at the University of Tampere, Finland.

Mamuka Tsurtsumia is PhD researcher of Medieval History at the Ivane Javakhishvili Tbilisi State University, Georgia.

1 Introduction

Felix Hinz and Johannes Meyer-Hamme

It was rather the conflict of opinion between Jews and Christians, as well as between Jews themselves, which compelled me to ponder the gaping discrepancy between what the National Socialists alleged concerning the Jews, and the image of Judaism as it presented itself to me. The contradictory teachings flowed over me wherever I went: at home, in the circles of the Jewish community and at school. To give but one example, within only a few years I had heard three different accounts of the history of the Crusades. The first portrayed the crusaders as the noble, proud army of Christendom, which set out to free the Holy Land from the clutches of unbelieving Muslims. At that time the history and reading books of the Prussian school system were still entirely within the Christian-Romantic tradition.

In the Jewish religious education we learned that the First Crusade was the prelude to horrific persecutions of the Jews. Wherever the crusader armies went – cobbled together from knights, adventurers, desperados and back-alley rabble – they left blood, smoke and ashes, in France, Germany, Hungary or the Holy Land itself. Our teachers emphasized that the then Pope, Urban II, remained silent about these atrocities. The first Crusaders had the opportunity to create the model for all further crusaders, as well as for the pogroms that would come later. This era marks the date of a deep alienation from which neither Jews nor Christians have been fully healed.

The third version we were taught was according to the redesigned curriculum that had been brought in line with National Socialism. The sermons on the Crusades, as elucidated by our brown uniformed history teacher, were only a means of harnessing the knighthood of the West for the Popes' "goals outside those of the national interest". In reality the Popes were not concerned with liberating the Tomb of Christ, but in expanding their own political power as well as plundering the fabulous riches of the East.[1]

This message by the Holocaust survivor Joel König serves as an example of how different the history of the Crusades can be interpreted. It is also an example of how intensely historical–political debates can be intertwined within a historical culture and history classes. The history of the Crusades in an international comparison is probably one of the most relevant subjects that continues to carry importance in a wide variety of contexts, despite the respective narratives fundamentally differing at times. The loss of Acre (1291), the last bastion of the crusader states in the Holy Land, was, and continues to be frequently presented as a significant historical break within the historiography of the Crusades. Although this date often was presented as the end of the Crusades, the idea was far from dead. The shadows of the Crusades still stretched long and far.[2] Public interest in the Crusades was often revived, not only during the time of colonialism, but also in the victory of the Allies over the Ottoman Empire and the accompanying British conquest of Jerusalem by General Allenby in 1917.[3] Moreover, the Crusades provide the basis for the founding myth of more than a few European states.[4] The USA, the 'nation with the soul of a church' (Gilbert Keith Chesterton), were in the particular position to repeatedly draw on the idea of the Crusades.[5] Since the 1990s, the topic has yet again become politically explosive. This is due to the reinvigoration of a political and aggressive form of Islam, as well as the realignment of the USA and the NATO to combat these forces.[6] In conjunction with the wars against the Taliban and al-Qaeda (2001), as well as the Iraq War (2003), there has been discussion of 'New Crusades'.[7] George W. Bush even referred to the latter explicitly as such. When it became clear that this type of rhetoric only played into the hands of Islamic propaganda, the West avoided using the concept of the Crusades at all costs. Yet, nothing had significantly changed; the West was even forced into a fight against the Islamic State.

The importance of the Crusades is also reflected in historical cultures. One example of this can be found in literature. For instance, between 1823 and 2014 in English, there were at least 274 historical novels published on the Crusades to the Orient. Even in 2013, there were at least 16 novels on the Crusades published, and 21 in 2014.[8] In the historical setting of the Holy City, it was not uncommon, during the respective formation period, to negotiate what be held as the final value for the society of the projected audience, and by which means one may or even must fight for it. The opinion forming power of the historical culture, to which state-regulated history classes belong, should not be underestimated. Although a respective academic level of knowledge is required, one should not forget that historians and teachers were and continue to be significantly influenced by the surrounding historical culture. Hence, the topic 'Crusades' has been highly controversial since the very appearance of the concept of a 'Crusade'.[9] The fact that history persists of historical narratives which vary according to the point of view was theoretically worked out in historiography (see Ch. 2) at least since the works of Johann Martin Chladenius (1710–1759). The question is *how* these narratives are constructed. What contextualization has been undertaken, and which interpretative frameworks are recognized and provide historical orientation? This list of questions could easily be enlarged. However, the focus of the current volume is not to work out the variety of the narratives that are cultivated within different societies. Instead, the focus is to present an international comparison of the dominant image of each respective historical culture and cultures of remembrance. It has to be kept in mind that countries should not be regarded as having one homogenous culture. Rather, they should be understood as not only synchronous, but also diachronic, multifaceted forms. Consequently, this implies historical narrations as well. Not only like the example in the introductory quote from Joel König demonstrates, but also as it plays out in the day-to-day within plural (migration-) societies. Notwithstanding, we decided to pursue an international comparison as a form of global history, in order to open up an overarching perspective for comparison.

At least within the West European historiography of the history of the Crusades, the British perspective currently dominates. Nevertheless, there are still large differences within European historical cultures, as the individual accounts in this volume (Ch. 3) display. We strove to compile this diversity, at least exemplarily. This is why we requested historians from different countries who work on the history of the Crusades and whose work meets Western academic standards to contribute. Most of these historians are located at a university.

However one arranges such a tableau, it must unavoidably remain incomplete. Yet when choosing the contributors, we were led by three aspirations: first, we wanted voices from hot-spots, i.e. from the frontlines of the history of the Crusades (viz. from the Middle East, the Baltic States and the Iberian Peninsula, as well as Malta). Second, we considered those places which represented the areas that constituted the numerically largest recruitment of crusaders (today France, Italy, Germany, England and the Benelux). Third, we wanted to look into those on the periphery (Norway) and even those behind the periphery (Ireland, Georgia, Russia, USA). In this way, we have 'victim perspectives' and 'perpetrator perspectives', 'key players' and 'minor players', as well as entirely different targets of the phenomenon.

All contributors were requested to answer two questions on only two pages:

- What were the Crusades?
- What do they mean for 'us' today?

It was important to us that the contributors did not answer these questions from a purely individual perspective. Instead, they were to provide answers that were relevant for a large group. Therefore, they were requested to support their reports with a few significant bibliographical references. That being said, it was not explicitly about merely comparing master narratives. To make this clear, we inserted a second French voice among the voices of the 26 different countries. Because most crusaders came from France and French vernaculars (the 'lingua franca') were the common language of the Crusader States, the French-speaking area carries a special importance for our question. The French contributors are both – like the majority of the others – seasoned historians with a large amount of experience and extensive knowledge about the Crusades. Here, it is by no means about establishing the worth or hierarchy among the individual texts. All are justified perspectives. The two French examples demonstrate that even historians in the same country – despite some obvious agreements – are by no means unified in their interpretations, and that controversy also exists within the same historical culture. Despite all the differences, we were aware that among all the points of views, the historians assembled are a part of a particular and international group: the scientific community. On the other hand, we determined that we would not grant any voices a platform that did not correspond to Western academic standards, and would therefore be classified as propaganda. Of course, these other voices exist alongside those depicted here – especially on the internet.

The way in which the 27 short narrations on the Crusades were compiled reveal, shared and conflicting memories of different groups. And these groups see themselves as heirs of the victims and observers, either positively as occupying heroes or negatively as occupying perpetrators of the Crusades. On the one hand, these self-assessments could change entirely in the course of time. On the other hand, there were lines of conflict that ran between the academics and the popular point of view within the respective groups. Nevertheless, in the context of each of these narrations – despite the attempt to provide a certain generally valid description of specific groups – they will always remain a subjective impression of the narrator.

This collection of short narratives offers extensive material on the Crusades as well as presenting, for present and later times, a rare and insightful profile of international, academic opinions on the Crusades. Proceeding in this manner, we might be able to substantially discuss four foundational questions:

1 Which forms of historical awareness within societies allow themselves to be differentiated for a comparison within an international perspective? In other words, in what way is the history of the Crusades in different historical cultures told? Which perspectives, interpretations and contemporary relevance can be distinguished and how are they to be explained (Ch. 2 and 3)?
2 What conclusions can be derived for the concept of historical learning in a globalized world from the variety of narratives? (Ch. 4)?
3 What pragmatic conclusions can be drawn for historical instruction in the classroom?
4 Which needs regarding empirical research on the Crusades become apparent?

Not least due to digital communication tools, it appears increasingly relevant within intercultural and transcultural discourse that not only historians reflect on the variety of narratives, but also that adolescents learn to constructively interact with this variety. With this background in mind, the collection presented here – with all the questions that are raised – could lay the foundation, in light of the current political state of the world, for important new discussions of the Crusades and their importance for 'us' today.

Notes

1 Joel König, *David. Aufzeichnungen eines Überlebenden (David. Records of a Survivor)* (Frankfurt a.M., 1979), pp. 52 f.
2 These self-assessments could entirely change in the course of time; however, at times lines of conflict ran between academics and popular opinion on the topic of Crusades within the relevant groups – Friedrich Heer, *Kreuzzüge – gestern, heute, morgen? (Crusades – Yesterday, Today, Tomorrow?)* (Luzern/Frankfurt a.M., 1969); Jonathan Riley-Smith, *The Crusades, Christianity, and Islam* (New York, 2008); Felix Hinz (ed.), *Kreuzzüge des Mittelalters und der Neuzeit. Realhistorie – Geschichtskultur – Didaktik (Crusades of the Middle Ages and in the Modern Era. History – Historical Culture – Didactics)* (Hildesheim, 2015).

3 F.H. Cooper, *Khaki Crusaders. With the South African Artillery in Egypt and Palestine* (Cape Town, 1919); Ralph Adams, *The Modern Crusaders* (London, 1920); Joseph Bowes, *The Aussie Crusaders. With Allenby in Palestine* (London, 1920) or John N. More, *With Allenby's Crusaders* (London, 1923).
4 Elizabeth Siberry, *The New Crusaders. Images of the Crusades in the Nineteenth and Early Twentieth Centuries* (Aldershot/Burlington USA/Singapore/Sydney, 2000); Ines-Anna Guhe, *Die Kreuzzüge narrativ inszeniert. Nationale und europäische Kreuzzugsrepräsentationen in französischen und deutschen Schulgeschichtsbüchern (1871–1914) (The Crusades Narratively Staged. National and European Crusade Representations in French and German History Textbooks (1871–1914))* (Münster, 2016).
5 Ernest Lee Tuveson, *Redeemer Nation: The Idea of America's Millennial Role* (Chicago, 1968); Joseph Dickman, *The Great Crusade. A Narrative on the World War* (New York/London, 1927); William Henry Chamberlin, *America's Second Crusade* (Chicago, 1950); Dwight D. Eisenhower, *Crusade in Europe* (New York, 1948); Gregory A. Daddis, *Fighting in the Great Crusade. An 8th Infantry Artillery Officer in World War II* (Baton Rouge, 2002); Paul Fussade, *The Boys' Crusade. The American Infantry in Northwestern Europe, 1944–1945* (New York, 2003); Hedley P. Willmott, *The Great Crusade* (London, 1989); Chester L. Cooper, *The Lost Crusade: The Full Story of US Involvement in Vietnam from Roosevelt to Nixon* (London, 1970).
6 Samuel Phillips Huntington, 'The Clash of Civilizations?', *Foreign Affairs* 73, 3 (Summer 1993), pp. 22–49.
7 Emran Qureshi and Michael A. Sells (eds.), *The New Crusades: Constructing the Muslim Enemy* (New York, 2003); Gilles Kepel, *Fitna: guerre au cœur de l'Islam (Fitna: War in the Heart of Islam)* (Paris, 2004); John Feffer, *Crusade 2.0. The West's Resurgent War against Islam* (San Francisco, 2012).
8 All of them listed in: Felix Hinz (ed.), *Kreuzzüge*, pp. 347–358. Also see: Felix Hinz, 'The Crusades in Literature, Film and Education', in *Cambridge History of the Crusades*, ed. Jonathan Phillips (Cambridge, forthcoming).
9 Christopher Tyerman, *The Debate on the Crusades* (Manchester, 2011).

2 Experts write about historical cultures – theoretical premises and methodological comments

Felix Hinz and Johannes Meyer-Hamme

The idea of a project of asking experts to compose characteristic stories of the history of the Crusades from differing historical cultures is based on historiographic-theoretical foundations that will be presented here. It is by no means surprising that they did not arrive at identical stories, a point already emphasized by Keith Jenkins.[1] A complete history of the Crusades void of perspective, one that would provide a one-to-one depiction of the past, is neither possible, nor is it useful, as already shown by Arthur C. Danto or Edward H. Carr.[2] Additionally, when there are attempts to refute these historiographic-theoretical premises,[3] they are unconvincing.[4] *History* is constitutively demarcated by *the past*. When this is acknowledged, the question is how historical phenomena should be recounted in historiography today, and how they are to be differentiated.

The following basic historiographic-theoretical considerations focus, as a first step, on a structural model of historical thinking, in order that the results might be made understandable. A second step situates this model in how societies deal with history, and utilizes the concept of *historical culture*, differentiating between five dimensions (see p. 15). In a third step, the methodological question is how, against the preceding background, the texts on historical cultures can be interpreted by the historians.

Moving on to historical thinking, the underlying assumption of this project was not *that* the narratives about the Crusades would fundamentally differ. (To this point, there are sufficient academic publications from differing perspectives.[5]) It is much more a question of *which* forms of historical narratives on the Crusades are there today, and what societal functions they serve. In the international comparison, it should be possible to discuss *how* these narratives are constructed. In most cases – but by no means in all – the result of requesting the authors to write a characteristic story of the historical cultures of their respective country resulted in the authors employing the concept of the nation as an interpretive framework. The recourse to the concept of the nation served as a tool to facilitate classification. Yet, it must be stressed that nations, in the sense according to Benedict Anderson, are to be understood as imagined communities,[6] whose narratives of the past are assigned a place of outstanding importance. It is not uncommon that the history of the Crusades plays a prominent role, which underscores the relevance of the project at hand. In connection to the Crusades, Kristin Skottki explicitly adapts the concept, 'identity machine' from Jeffrey Jerome Cohen.[7] It is not rare for such stories to be invented and has already been repeatedly researched.[8] Such instances will also be clearly seen in some examples of the present study.

Furthermore, as formerly stated, it should be taken into account that nations – as imagined communities – should not be seen as homogenous unities that can be clearly demarcated from each other and foster a distinct and unified view of history within their respected demarcated zones. Much more it is about the connection of diverse forms of historical culture, so that the differing cultures overlap. Nations are not to be understood as essentialistic entities, but as efficacious cultural constructions of communities.[9] At the same time, one must keep in mind that such constructs are historically developed and have frequently led to wars and conflicts. Due to this – also in light of post-national structures online – the question of post-national practices and constructs of identity will be discussed. These are independent of national boundaries and will be thought of and treated beyond them.[10] The international comparison certainly takes into account that history is often told from the perspective of a nation-state. It should not be forgotten that the brevity of the requested texts leads to the dominant views of the Crusades being mentioned – whereas the differentiation of the societal varieties in dealing with this history remains largely concealed.

The international comparison of dominant historical narratives is justified in that historical instruction is, in many cases, conceived of and conducted within a national context – i.e. in school. Therefore, not only must the differing forms of historical narration that appear be made clear, but also – utilizing the examples provided here – to discuss how history lessons might be conceived of in a globalized world.[11] Specifically, how might this be done when – and this has already been anticipated – the narratives provided here radically differ from each other.[12]

We use an understanding of history that is chiefly based on the work of Arthur Danto[13] and Jörn Rüsen,[14] as well as post-modern historical theory[15] and post-colonial inquiry underlies this line of questioning.

According to Danto, every historical narrative is to be understood as a retrospective and particular narration presenting a specific way of clarifying the present. Therefore, history is not to be equated with the past. Instead, it is always tied to some present attribution of meaning, which is derived from selected statements on the past. And these must be evaluated according to their meaning for the present. These types of relevance allocations are made with a view towards future expectations, making orientation in the course of time both plausible and possible. This was worked out by Jörn Rüsen.[16] History is, then, to be understood as the 'construction of meaning by the experience of time', by establishing a complex of meaning that begins with contemporary questions about the past with a view towards the future – even if the future references often remain implicit. This becomes clear when history is narrated in such a way that the origins of contemporary traditions are remembered, or timeless rules are derived ('historia magistra vitae'), although it must be accepted that the traditions and rules are valid in the future. However, it is also possible to narrate developments which extend into the future and look different from the past. Jörn Rüsen differentiated these three foundational forms of historical constructions of meaning. He designated them as *traditional*, *exemplary* and *genetic* narratives. The assumption is made that such constructs of meaning are valid for every historical narration, although they are often not carried out explicitly and remain implicit (in that some type of origin is recalled without reference to future validity claims). There are still other ways of understanding history which reject traditional, exemplary and genetic constructs of meaning without offering an alternative. Rüsen describes these as *critical* constructs of meaning.[17] Rarely does this form of a construct of meaning appear in historical narrations in its pure form. The longer and the more complex the narrations, the more diverse the combinations can usually be determined. Andreas Körber explicitly applied Rüsen's model of patterns of meaning construction to the history of the Crusades and continued to differentiate. Essentially, his endeavours tie into our first question, 'What were the Crusades?' and outline a diagram of possible answers:

In this manner, the functions of historical narratives can be described. The process of historical thinking can be more specifically differentiated through the metaphor of a regulator circuit (Figure 2.1). The starting point of historical thinking is according to (1) the need for orientation in time, for instance, when changes or conditions require clarification. The answers to the need for orientation involve historical narratives, as described by Danto. They are always bound to the present (thereby also oriented towards the future), and are only

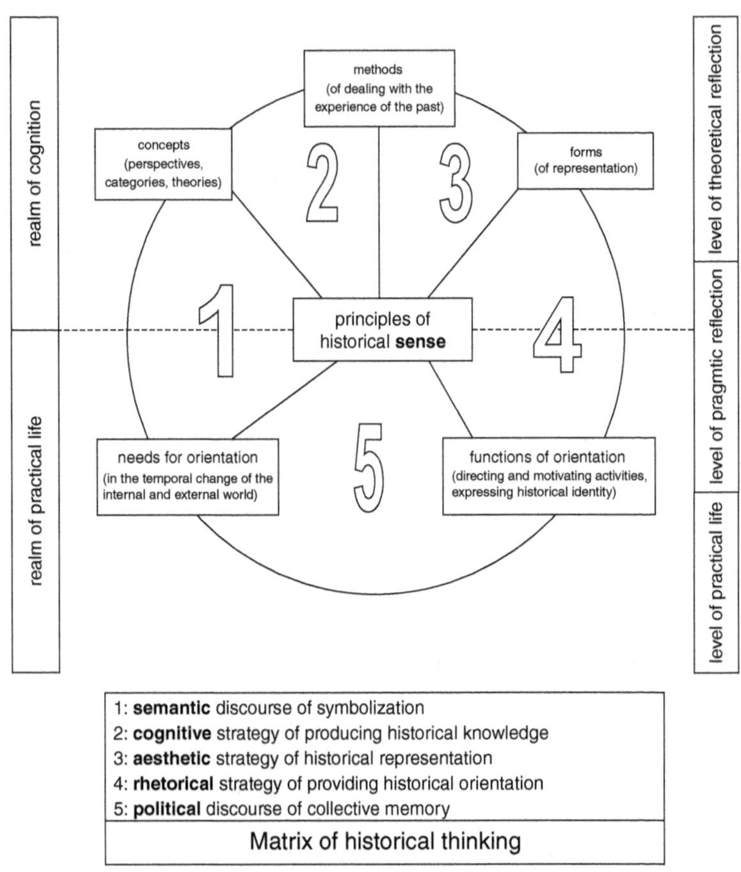

Figure 2.1 Matrix of historical thinking (Rüsen 2017, p. 43).[18]

retrospective in light of being led by these interests. In the context of the Crusades, it might be asked which present-day societal and political interests move towards the focus of attention and encourage historical narration.

In these historical narrations, (2) the *concepts* of the historians are taken as a guiding perspective of which experiences of the past are to be included, e.g. whether or not the Crusades are generally to be interpreted by religious, political, economic or entirely different categories, which leads to different sources depending on the decision made. These premises are to be understood as necessary conditions that make possible a useful selection of potential ways to engage with the past. Every engagement with the past is necessarily from a specific perspective and, at the same time, beholden to theoretical premises. In this way, theoretical assumptions go down in history, with which phenomena of the past are explained.

Included in constructing historical narratives are (3) *methods* of acquiring knowledge that are regulated by historiography (even though the respective methods are being discussed), but applied to other forms of historical thinking in their unregulated form. Of note is the treatment of historical sources, which never possess a complete depiction of the past, but can always only be a partial remnant of it. And it is from these incomplete remnants that the historian must choose his corpus. All historical thinking is characterized by partiality and selectivity. Hence, the interests and ideas of the historian characterize the selection and designation of persons and/or events. Even at this level, always already present-day interpretations flow into historiography.[19] In the context of the Crusades, the question must be raised as to where and how (and in which language) the source material has been handed down and underlies historical research, as well as which sources were selected from this pool of material. It is especially important to keep in mind that it is not by accident that, to this day, most of the standard editions of crusader history were published in the time of imperialism and colonialism in France and in the French language.[20]

The results of the empirical research are historical narrations. They can take the (4) *form* of a presentation (be it a non-fiction book or a historical film), provided that typical characteristics are always included in the narrative. Historical thinking is, fundamentally, narrative; it presents a linguistic linking of details in relation to the past, details which contain a retrospective attribution of significance.[21] Each of these presentations is provisional and hypothetical. They change in the course of time and in their dependence on theoretical premises and perspectives. In the context of the history of the Crusades, one might ask which different categories exist (e.g. academic literature, historical novels, political speeches, historical monuments), and what effects they evoke.

Finally, historical narratives perform (5) the *function of orientation*, namely, that of orienting in one's own life. They do this by offering a construct of meaning originating from the temporal need for orientation. These are written for specific addressees as described earlier. In this respect, history is identity-related and part of building meaning.[22] It is hardly worth mentioning that the metaphor of the circle does not imply that at the end of historical thinking, the point of origin will be attained. However, the construction of meaning does relate to the interest for knowledge of the origin.

The previously mentioned distinction between the past and history can now be more precisely clarified. Every history can be identified by certain structural characteristics. History is a narrative that is bound to the present, bound to theory and a partial selective perspective. It is always an answer referring to a historical question that is provisional, identity-related and constructs meaning (see Table 2.1)

The structural characteristics of historical thinking concern necessary conditions that make historical knowledge possible in the first place. Yet for this very reason, they require reflection and should not be investigated to overcome deficient characteristics. For as already Arthur Danto shows in his thought experiment of the omniscient chronicler, nothing could be done with a complete and neutral ('objective') representation of the past. This is because it alone did not make possible the construction of meaning by the abundance of information unnecessary in the present.[23] Only through selection and attributing importance does history become relevant for the present.

Provided these considerations apply, the following questions regarding the history of the Crusades within the context of historical cultures might be asked:

1 Which present-day interests and functions of the narrative for the present are identifiable?
2 Which concepts and forms of historical interpretation exist?
3 Which results of empirical research, that is, which concrete references to the past[24] have been selected and designated?

If the history of the Crusades, in their completely different forms, is now going to be dealt with in the public sphere, then, in this context, the question of how the findings of considerably different narratives are to be evaluated must be discussed. Here, the question of historical truth is raised. The above-mentioned book by Richard Evans, *In Defence of History*, assumes that historical facts are independent of historians and can be reconstructed through the use of primary sources. According to Evans, the sources 'speak' to historians, and from this basis, assertions about the past can be made.[25] If this position (one rarely held today) were valid, there would need to be a significant agreement in narratives on the Crusades, and differences would need to be clarified by the partiality of historical transmission.

Keith Jenkins takes up a counter position, whose argument relates to Hayden White.[26] He argues that the question of which history will be recognized as plausible in the present is solely dependent upon the plot structure and its recognition.[27] In the context of this project, the

Table 2.1 Constructions of meaning of the Crusades (F. Hinz and J. Meyer-Hamme based on A. Körber)[28]

	Constructs of meaning			
	Factual-traditional	**Normative-traditional**	**Exemplary**	**Genetic**
Generally	It is assumed that underlying the superficial changes of external forms there is a normative as well as factual continuation of earlier constellations, interests and actions.	It is assumed that even with an interruption or cessation of activities, the intrinsic interests and conditions persist, so that a resumption of former activities is supported.	It is postulated that 'Crusades' are ('merely') an example for an overarching type of conflict. Hence crusade and counter-crusade ('jihad') – as well as structurally similar examples – can be evaluated from a common point of view.	It is assumed that norms, as well as circumstances and forms underlie foundational transformations. […]
Affirmative	• The idea of continuous (never ending) Crusades and jihadist propaganda as a counter-crusade [or other forms of fighting against 'Crusades']. • White racist 'Knights Templar ideology'.		• Transferring the thinking of Crusade to that of a new (worldly) evil. • Propaganda for 'Crusades' against 'Marxism' or the like.	Emphasizing (one's own) continued development with respect to former interests and methods.
Critical	• Rejecting the Islamic view concerning the presence of 'Western' groups and actors in the Middle East (bin Laden; Hamas). • Rejecting of right wing's idea of continuous confrontation between Islam and Europe.		The rejecting of the interpretation of the Crusades as an example of an underlying and continuing tradition that brings forth similar phenomena only under altered conditions. For instance, Deschner's interpretation of the Crusades as an example of a continuous 'criminal history' of Christianity.[29]	Rejecting the idea of (one's own) continued development with respect to former interests and methods.

heterogeneous findings present a fundamental problem to the position of Evans. Yet in the view of Jenkins, the findings would be described as a normal case.

Jörn Rüsen takes up a middle position, yet again offering criteria with which the plausibility of historical narrations might be evaluated. He starts with the assumption that history can be recognized as 'true' by asking the following four questions:

a To what degree can the 'facts' asserted by the history ('occurrences', 'people') be traced back to credible sources ('empirical plausibility')?
b To what degree are the theoretical premises credible ('theoretical plausibility')?
c To what degree do the constructs of meaning fit into the normative horizon of the addressees ('normative plausibility')?
d Is the narrative coherence between these aspects persuasive ('narrative plausibility')?[30]

In the present work, we asked for typical narratives and patterns of interpretation, that is, ones that are accepted in specific historical cultures. We asked for socially conventional interpretations that did not necessarily have to correspond to the author's own position. If the narratives about the Crusades fundamentally differ within the historical cultures,[31] then they are not valid in the same way for the recipients who are bound to a location and, therefore, are able to take a subjective perspective. Consequently, *it is not possible to provide a singular account of history (of the Crusades).*

Against this background, the specific question arises concerning how historical learning might be advantageously conceived under these conditions (Ch. 5).

However, there is another point that should be added. The three fundamental questions mentioned earlier are not sufficient for an analysis of historical cultures. Rather, it must be asked how a 'historical culture' can be more precisely understood.

> Historical culture is the product of our historical consciousness and its power to form meaning. It contains the cultural practice of the orientation of human action and suffering in time. Historical culture localizes human beings in the temporal changes under which they suffer and in which they must act and that are in turn (partly) determined and enforced by human action and suffering. The orientation achieved by historical culture is our

> way of interpreting our experience with the human past so that we can understand the present as well as develop strategies for the future.[32]

Thus, according to Rüsen, the concept 'historical culture' means the framework wherein entirely different ways of engaging with the past and history exist – from the scientific, to politics and even recreational activities. However, all of these are expressions of a collective structure of historical thinking. If this is in fact the case, then the texts presented here can be consulted as to how the history of the Crusades is narrated within the different historical cultures. Many of the authors chose to utilize academic as well as political and/or popular sources.[33] Therefore, in the context of a comprehensive historical culture, the question arises regarding the nature of the relationship between the academic historiography and non-academic work pertaining to the past and history. However, there is often not a clear-cut division between the two. Not only according to Rüsen (and also according to our understanding), it is necessary to consider historiography as a part of the respective historical cultures, because the need for orientation and the orienting functions of history are necessarily embedded in social experience and discourse. This is not to say that scientific historiography should be equated with other institutions. Instead, the primary function of historiography is to level criticism on the narratives of the past that have been offered until now, that is, to test the plausibility of existing narratives.[34] Rüsen differentiates five dimensions of historical culture. Although these dimensions can be considered individually, in reality they are interwoven.

- The *cognitive* dimension depicts the argumentative encounter with history. This dimension is focused on instances where the question of how historical statements can be justified is being answered. Admittedly, it must be taken into account that history cannot be proven, but only made plausible. That is, it can be considered preliminarily valid. When an orienting function is to be derived from history, it must be sufficiently justified for the relevant groups. Providing such justifications is a proprium of historiography. Rüsen metaphorically describes this 'consensual objectivity' with the term 'truth'. This dimension is often presupposed. Seldom are new sources explicitly discussed in society. As an example, reference can be made to the work of Kristin Skottki, wherein the selections and translations of the current source editions on the First Crusade are critically analysed in detail.[35]

- The *aesthetic* dimension describes how history needs its narrative structure to be formed, so that it might be told well and thereby persuasively apprehended. This is also a basic criterion for apprehending a specific history as relevant for one's orientation. This can be particularly observed in the case of historical novels as the aesthetic dimension plays a prominent role. Yet, this applies to all other forms of history. In the context of the history of the Crusades, this dimension clarifies the success of certain historical novels. One can point to Walter Scott's foundational novel, *The Talisman* (1825) – once consequential for politicians and historians. To this day, *The Talisman* continues to find readers and can be obtained in many different languages.[36]
- The *political* dimension focuses on the question of the legitimacy of specific, present-day political claims that use narratives as a means of affirmation. A narrative can only be relevant for orientation if the question of its legitimacy can be taken to be credible. At times, this question is explicitly asked. This dimension dominates when the legitimacy of rulers and their deeds is questioned. Yet, this dimension is always present in every narrative which speaks of human actions and sufferings. The political dimension can be frequently observed in the narratives of the Crusades. It is particularly evident when a continuation of the Crusades is postulated for today.[37]
- The *moral* dimension focuses on how the question of good and evil is raised. A narrative can only be convincing and relevant for orientation if the moral dimension in a narrative can be apprehended as convincing. At times, this question prevails, such as when particularly immoral deeds are brought into focus (e.g. the massacre by the crusaders during the first conquest of Jerusalem in 1099).[38] The moral dimension is also present when especially virtuous conduct of historical role models is told. Since the Enlightenment (Lessing), this was done predominately in respect to the ideas of Sultan Saladin. He was regarded as a virtuous ruler beyond religious and political boundaries, having 'legitimately' reconquered Jerusalem.[39]
- The *religious* dimension plays a role for history where faith as a criterion of meaning is addressed. In this way, the history of the Crusades can be told from the basis of a religious, or explicitly non-religious, interpretive framework. In Osama bin Laden's interpretations of history, for example, the question of salvation was of vital importance.[40]

The discussion within history didactics of whether or not these dimensions are exhaustive (e.g. should an economic dimension be added) is relevant for theory. However, they will not be addressed in the present study. The fundamental, and for this book, most important thesis of Rüsen is that history is only socially relevant for orientation if it does not stand in contradiction to any of the five dimensions. At the same time, often within public discourse, when the question of the relevance for orientation is discussed, only a single dimension dominates the discussion. It is also worth questioning which dimensions are described within the texts on historical culture.

Against this background, a fourth question can be formulated:

4 To what extent can the descriptions of historical cultures be more precisely characterized in these five different dimensions?

The final question to be discussed is what assertions are possible based on the texts on historical cultures presented here. These texts are written by historians, as experts, about historical cultures. Building from this basis, historical cultures can be compared insofar as the dominant narratives are perceived therein, as well as which media and actors from the historical culture are mentioned. The brevity of the texts inevitably leaves many subjects related to the Crusades unmentioned. It must be assumed that there is a plethora of subject matter that makes multifaceted and overlapping discoveries possible. Focusing on the dominant narratives allows for an initial look at the history of the Crusades from an international comparison in a shortened form. This involves looking at which interpretations of the Crusades are socially recognized as well as which interpretations of the Crusades are to be considered conventions for dealing with history. Such conventions of historical thinking are relevant for the construction of historical educational programmes.[41]

Finally, it is important to provide some comments regarding our methodology. The evaluation (Ch. 4) is based on a qualitative analysis of the content presented in the texts.[42] The central idea belonging to this method of interpretation is that the texts are compared on the level of explicit statements and that continued interpretation and contextualization does not take place (unless in cases that appear particularly important to the editors, and then within the footnotes). The texts will not be subjected to a plausibility analysis with regard to empirical evidence, theoretical premises, normative statements and narrative coherence. Rather, dimensions in the narratives of historical cultures will be pointed out, and show to what extent they are similar, resemble each other, are different or contradictory. An analysis of the reasons for, and the question of, which of these narratives appear plausible and relevant for orientation is left up to the readers, for whom the narratives cannot be equally plausible.

Only historians whom we take seriously as experts in respect to cultures of remembrance were asked to contribute. We explicitly did not ask how they orient themselves within historical cultures and how they assess the plausibility of the dominant narratives in society. Statements about the historical consciousness of the authors could at best be observed implicitly and are not intended to be made in this project. Details and contextualization will only be added by the editors in order to further understanding and subsequent interpretation (Ch. 4).

Despite these constraints, the present project offers an initial international comparative view, in a shortened form, of the reception of the Crusades within historical cultures. The different interpretations in their respective political, historical and cultural relevance will become apparent so that, from this background, the question of historical learning within a globalized world can be discussed.

Notes

1 Keith Jenkins, *Rethinking History* (London, 2004), pp. 6–32.
2 Edward H. Carr, *What Is History?* (Middlesex, 1961); Arthur C. Danto, *Analytical Philosophy of History* (Cambridge, 1965).
3 Richard J. Evans, *In Defence of History* (London, 1997), pp. 75–77.
4 Otto Gerhard Oexle, 'Im Archiv der Fiktionen', in *Auf der Suche nach der verlorenen Wahrheit. Zum Grundlagenstreit in der Geschichtswissenschaft (In Search of the Lost Truth. On the Fundamental Dispute in Historical Science)*, eds. Rainer Maria Kiesow, Dieter Simon (Frankfurt a.M., 2000), pp. 87–103.
5 F.e. Amin Maalouf, *The Crusades through Arab Eyes* (London, 1984); Mikolaj Gladysz, *The Forgotten Crusaders. Poland and the Crusader Movement in the Twelfth and Thirteenth Centuries* (Leiden, 2012); Jonathan M. Harris, *Byzantium and the Crusades* (London, 2014); Felix Hinz (ed.), *Kreuzzüge des Mittelalters und der Neuzeit. Realhistorie – Geschichtskultur – Didaktik. (Crusades of the Middle Ages and in the Modern Era. History – Historical Culture – Didactics)* (Hildesheim, 2015); Jaap van Moolenbroek, *Nederlandse kruisvaarders naar Damiate aan de Nijl, acht eeuwen geschiedenis en fantasie in woord en beel (Dutch Crusaders at Damietta on the Nile, Eight Centuries of History and Fantasy in Word and Image)* (Hilversum, 2016); Megan Cassidy-Welch (ed.), *Remembering the Crusades and Crusading* (London/New York, 2017); Luigi Russo, *I crociati in Terrasanta: una nuova storia (1095–1291) (The Crusaders in the Holy Land: A New History (1095–1291))* (Rome, 2018), and many others.
6 Benedict Anderson, *Imagined Communities: Reflections on the Origin and Spread of Nationalism* (London/Frankfurt a.M., 2006).

7 Kristin Skottki, *Christen, Muslime und der Erste Kreuzzug. Die Macht der Beschreibung in der mittelalterlichen und modernen Historiographie (Christians, Muslims and the First Crusade. The Power of Description in Medieval and Modern Historiography)* (Münster/New York, 2015), p. 488.
8 F.e. Elizabeth Siberry, *The New Crusaders. Images of the Crusades in the 19th and early 20th Centuries* (Aldershot/Burlington, 2000); Nikolas Jaspert, 'Die Kreuzzüge und ihre Deutungen: Mythen und Motivationen' (The Crusades and their Interpretations: Myths and Motivations), in *Stauferzeit – Zeit der Kreuzzüge (Time of the Staufer – Time of the Crusades)*, ed. Karl-Heinz Rueß (Göppingen, 2011), pp. 10–41; Megan Cassidy-Welch (ed.), *Remembering*; Nicholas Paul and Suzanne Yeager (eds.), *Remembering the Crusades. Myth, Image, and Identity.* (Baltimore, 2012); Mike Horswell and Jonathan Phillips (eds.), *Perceptions of the Crusades from the Nineteenth to the Twenty-First Century* (Engaging the Crusades; 1) (London/New York, 2018) and others.
9 See Chapters 3 and 4.
10 Sina Arnold, Sebastian Bischoff, Jana König, 'Postnationale Potenziale. Praktiken jenseits der Nation' (Postnational Potentials. Practices Beyond Nation), *Aus Politik und Zeitgeschichte* 48 (2018), pp. 27–33.
11 See Chapter 5.
12 See Chapter 5.
13 Arthur C. Danto, *Analytical Philosophy.*
14 F.e. Jörn Rüsen, *Historische Vernunft. Grundzüge einer Historik I: Die Grundlagen der Geschichtswissenschaft (Historical Reason. Fundamentals of a Theory of History I: The Foundations of Historical Science)* (Göttingen, 1983).
15 F.e. Keith Jenkins, *Rethinking History.*
16 Jörn Rüsen, *Historische Vernunft.*
17 Jörn Rüsen, *Evidence and Meaning: A Theory of Historical Studies* (New York, 2017), pp. 157–167.
18 Ibid. p. 43. Figure reproduced by permission of Berghahn Books.
19 To this question, see: Keith Jenkins, *Rethinking History*, pp. 6–32.
20 Kristin Skottki, *Christen*, pp. 184–189.
21 Arthur Danto, *Analytical Philosophy.*
22 Jörn Rüsen, *Historische Vernunft*, p. 16.
23 Arthur Danto, *Analytical Philosophy*, pp. 241–243.
24 Since the focus is on the product of historical thinking, and not the process of it, the methods cannot be questioned; yet, the decisions relating to the selection and definition of persons and events that were made on the basis of the methods can be questioned.
25 Richard J. Evans, *In Defence*, pp. 75–128.
26 Hayden White, *Metahistory: The Historical Imagination in Nineteenth-Century Europe* (Baltimore, 1973).
27 Keith Jenkins, *Refiguring History* (London, 2003), pp. 33–58.
28 Andreas Körber, 'Die Kreuzzüge – ein ergiebiges Thema für (interkulturelles) historisches Lernen?' (The Crusades – A Profitable Subject for (Intercultural) Historical Learning?), in *Kreuzzüge des Mittelalters*, ed. Felix Hinz, pp. 285–320, here: p. 295.

29 Karlheinz Deschner, *Kriminalgeschichte des Christentums (Criminal History of Christendom)*, vol. 6: *11. und 12. Jahrhundert: Von Kaiser Heinrich II., dem 'Heiligen' (1002), bis zum Ende des Dritten Kreuzzugs (1192) (11th and 12th Centuries: From Emperor Henry II, the 'Saint' (1002), to the end of the Third Crusade (1192))* (Reinbek, 1999), pp. 339–384.
30 Jörn Rüsen, *Evidence and Meaning*, pp. 36–40.
31 See Chapters 3 and 4.
32 Jörn Rüsen, *Evidence and Meaning*, p. 168.
33 See Chapters 3 and 4.
34 Jörn Rüsen, *Evidence and Meaning*, p. 186.
35 Kristin Skottki, *Christen*, p. 488.
36 Felix Hinz, *Mythos Kreuzzüge. Selbst- und Fremdbilder in historischen Romanen, 1786–2012 (The Myth of the Crusades. Images of oneself and of others in historical novels, 1786–2012)* (Schwalbach/Ts., 2014).
37 F.e. Emran Qureshi and Michael A. Sells (eds.), *The New Crusades: Constructing the Muslim Enemy* (New York, 2003); Gilles Kepel, *Fitna: guerre au cœur de l'Islam (Fitna: War in the Heart of Islam)* (Paris, 2004); John Feffer, *Crusade 2.0. The West's Resurgent War against Islam* (San Francisco, 2012).
38 F.e. Amin Maalouf, *The Crusades Through Arab Eyes* (London, 1984).
39 See Hannes Möhring, *Saladin. Der Sultan und seine Zeit, 1138–1193 (Saladin. The Sultan and his Time, 1138–1193)* (Munich, 2012), chap. 7; Felix Hinz, *Mythos Kreuzzüge*, pp. 78–86; Mohamed El-Moctar, 'Saladin in Sunni and Shi'a Memories', in *Remembering the Crusades. Myth, Image, and Identity*, eds. Nicholas Paul and Suzanne Yeager (Baltimore, 2012), pp. 197–214 or Jonathan Phillips, *The Life and Legend of Sultan Saladin* (London, 2019).
40 Osama Bin Laden, 'Zweiter Brief an die Muslime im Irak. Abschrift einer aufgezeichneten Erklärung Bin Ladens, die am 18. Oktober 2003 verbreitet wurde zusammen mit einer zweiten, an die Amerikaner gerichteten Botschaft' (Second letter to the Muslims in Iraq. Transcript of a recorded statement of Bin Laden circulated on 18th of October 2003 along with a second message addressed to the Americans), in *Al-Qaida. Texte des Terrors (Al-Qaida. Texts of Terror)*, eds. Gilles Kepel and Jean-Pierre Milelli (Munich/Zurich, 2006), pp. 119–124, here: p. 120.
41 See Chapter 5.
42 Udo Kuckartz, *Qualitative Text Analysis. Methods, Practice, Computer Assistance* (London, 2014).

3 International views on the Crusades

3.1 The ambiguous memory of Norwegian crusading – a view from Norway

Kristin B. Aavitsland

According to medieval sources from Scandinavia, continental Europe and the Arab world, Norwegians participated in Levantine crusading to a certain extent, especially during the 12th century. The first armed expedition from Norway to Palestine appears to have been a small group of noblemen departing in 1102, most of them never to return. Five years later, the Norwegian king Sigurd Magnusson went on a campaign with a large fleet of crusaders. He reached Palestine in 1111 and offered military support to the Frankish kingdom of Jerusalem. King Sigurd's expedition earned him the epithet 'Jerusalem-traveller' or simply 'Crusader' (*Jórsalafari*). Minor expeditions left Norway and the Norwegian settlement at Orkney in the following decades. In 1153, a new campaign, this time on a larger scale, was organized by Rognvald, Earl of Orkney, and the magnate Erling Ormson, King Sigurd's son-in-law. Furthermore, a group of Norwegian magnates appears to have joined the Danes in their unsuccessful participation in the Third Crusade. In the 13th century, two more kings took up crusading. King Inge II Bårdsson equipped a large fleet but died before it left in 1217. In the 1250s, King Haakon IV Haakonson was involved in international negotiations on crusading, but he never went to the Levant.

Generally, the role of Norway in the history of the Crusades (in Norwegian *korstog*, cf. German *Kreuzzüge*) does not loom large in the country's collective memory. The only exception is the crusader King Sigurd Magnusson, who was surrounded by a certain heroic aura during the 19th and early 20th centuries. This period was characterized by an ongoing process of building a new national identity, which conditioned the perception of Norway's medieval kings. The prevailing narrative of the country's history was construed according to the three-stage pattern of a classical myth. The first phase was a long-past golden age (the Middle

Ages, when Norway was an independent and expansive kingdom); in the second phase came 'the dark ages' and suppression under the foreign rule (when Norway became a dependency under Denmark from 1380 to 1814); and eventually a new awakening and liberation arrived (the constitution of 1814 and subsequent independence from Sweden in 1905). King Sigurd the Crusader belonged to the heroic age of independence and expansion, and his Crusade was interpreted in this light. In 1872, the extremely influential author and playwright Bjørnstjerne Bjørnson (1832–1910) staged a piece about the crusader king, with music composed by the celebrated national romantic composer Edvard Grieg (1843–1907). The performance was a great success. Twenty years later, painter and designer Gerhard Munthe (1849–1929) had two large *art nouveau* tapestries made with scenes from King Sigurd's expedition. The national prestige of these tapestries was evident from the fact that they were exhibited at the Paris Universal Exhibition in 1900. And five years later, when Norway regained its independence after the dissolution of the union with Sweden, the crusader tapestries were given to King Haakon VII, the first monarch of an independent Norway since the Middle Ages.

The ideological undertones in Munthe's tapestries are clearly nationalistic, celebrating the glory of fame, heroic bravery and national pride. In Bjørnson's play, however, the glorious king emerges more ambivalent. Allegedly, Sigurd suffered from sporadic seizures of madness, and Bjørnson construes this as a trauma caused by his expedition. The play ends with the king rejecting new crusading endeavours and leaving his ambitions of mission and national expansion. Instead, he turns to domestic affairs and the task of cultivating his country. The Crusade obviously had no clear ideological value in Bjørnson's nation building literary works.

A similar tendency to focus on domestic issues and leave international topics like crusading out of sight can also be found in Norwegian historiography in the 19th, 20th and even 21st centuries. The relatively rich source material on Norwegians and the Crusades has been largely unexplored. It is characteristic that, until quite recently, the only comprehensive academic study of Norwegian involvement and participation in the Crusades was written by a Frenchman: Count Paul Riant, who submitted his vast survey of crusading Scandinavians in medieval sources as a doctoral dissertation at Sorbonne in 1865. In most studies of Norwegian medieval history, the Crusades are mentioned only in passing or anecdotally, if at all. In textbooks on national history, the Crusades are barely present. The pronounced increase in interest for local Crusade history that can be observed in Sweden and Denmark seems not to have reached Norway.

Reasons for this lack of interest, despite the richness of source material, may be multiple. In the 19th and early 20th centuries, there was a nationalistic disinterest in the European (Catholic) influence on the medieval kingdom of Norway. Moreover, Norwegian historiography has long been dominated by a Marxist approach, with an emphasis on materialism and economic resources rather than ideology, religion and ideas.

A shift, however, may be seen in the early 21st century. There is a tendency among a new generation of historians to delve into the long-neglected body of source material. In the public sphere, the former nationalistic heroism has given way to a post-colonial approach, wherein the Muslim perspective on crusading history is favoured and often idealized. In 2004, the author Thorvald Steen (born 1954) published a novel about Saladin, offering a flattering portrait of the Kurdish warlord as a spokesman for religious tolerance. Starting in 2009, the international Saladin-days have been organized in Oslo, an annual festival dedicated to political and religious dialogue, literature, debates and lectures, often with a focus on Middle East culture.

Antagonistic to these initiatives, other references to the Crusades can be found on the far right. Norway's relatively modest Crusade history was ideologically used – or rather abused. In 2011, Norway suffered a horrible terrorist attack from a right-wing extremist who bombed the governmental quarter in Oslo and massacred 77 young people at a political summer camp. Claiming to fight for Norwegian and Christian values against left-wing decadence and Muslim immigration, the terrorist posted a 1,500-page manifesto in which he construed himself as a modern crusader, taking the name of the Norwegian crusader king, Sigurd Jerusalem-Traveller. Medievalists publicly rejected this illegitimate application of the historical past.

Literature

Bjørnson, Bjørnstjerne. *Sigurd Jorsalfar* (Sigurd the Crusader). Copenhagen, 1872.

Oftestad, Eivor A. «Historiske og konstruerte korsfarere» (Historical and fictitious crusaders), *Minerva*, August 12, 2011 (www.minervanett.no/historiske-og-konstruerte-korsfarere/).

Riant, Paul E. D. *Expéditions et pèlerinages des Scandinaves en Terre Sainte au temps des croisades (Expeditions and Pilgrimages of the Scandinavians to the Holy Land During the Crusades)*. Paris, 1865.

Svenungsen, Pål Berg. *Norge og korstogene: En studie av forbindelsene mellom det norske riket og den europeiske korstogsbevegelsen, ca. 1050–1380 (Norway and the Crusades: A Study of the Connections between the Norwegian Realm and the European Crusade Movement, ca. 1050–1380)*. Bergen, 2016.

Svenungsen, Pål Berg. 'The Saint and the Wry-neck - Norse Crusaders and a Jerusalem in the North'. In K. B. Aavitsland and L.M. Bonde (eds), *The Holy City: Tracing the Jerusalem Code, Vol. 1 Christian Cultures in Medieval Scandinavia (c. 1000–1536)*. Berlin: De Gruyter, 2020.

3.2 'Frankish invasions' and 'a cosmic struggle between Islam and Christianity' – a view from Jordan

Mazhar Al-Zo'by

The Crusades and their broader impact (i.e. military, religious, economic and cultural) on the Arab Middle East have occupied a central status in school curriculum and popular imagination in Jordan. As they were referred to in medieval Islamic historiography (see Ali Ibn al-Athir, for example), contemporary texts in Jordan refer to the Crusades as the 'Frankish Invasions' (hurub al-faranga). This is because the term 'farang' (or Franj) was widely used to refer to Westerners. The official narratives about the Crusades as expressed in school curricula in Jordan largely focus on the military, economic and geo-strategic features of these campaigns, placing less emphasis on the religious dimensions of the invasions. Although the crusader campaigns are framed as Christian holy wars to capture Jerusalem, official textbooks in Jordan predominantly focus on the economic and geographic significance of the country for the Crusade and anti-Crusade battles. For example, the textbooks contain detailed descriptions of the geo-strategic significance of southern Jordan for the Crusades. Stressing the central location of historic Jordan, textual accounts are provided as to why the Crusades needed to build monumental castles and forts in order to maintain military, economic and communication control of the area. For instance, by constructing one of the largest castles in the Levant, the Kerak Castle (constructed around 1142 and called Crac des Moabites by the crusaders), and Shoubak Castle (constructed around 1115, and called by the Crusades Montreal Castle). The crusaders used southern Jordan to control the frankincense and myrrh trade routes between southern Arabia and the north routes. Furthermore, they were able to impose taxation on all merchant caravans and, most importantly, prevented all communication between Egypt and the Levant region. Similarly, official textbooks in Jordan focus with great detail on why the legendary figure of Saladin (Salah ad-Din ibn Ayyub 1137–1193, founder of the Ayyubid Dynasty) focused on Jordan as well as on his campaigns to recapture Jerusalem from the crusaders (the Second Crusade). Emphasizing parallel geographic and military advantages, official textbooks in Jordan highlight why he sought to capture Kerak and Shoubak from the crusaders, for instance, in order to gain full control of the area. Moreover, the textual accounts of the these campaigns illustrate the significance of Northern Jordan as an area that allowed even more strategic control both of the Holy Land and the trade routes in the Levant, explaining why some castles were constructed in that area (the Ajloun Castle, in particular).

Official narratives furthermore focus on how the Ayyubid victory over the crusaders revived the educational system (by establishing schools in the region), economic prosperity (by securing trade routes) and the agricultural sector (by alleviating taxation), all of which augments the glory and marvel of the legendary figure of Saladin and his historic legacy for Islam and Muslims.

While official narratives in Jordan focus primarily on the military, economic and geographic aspects of the Crusades and counter Crusades campaigns, popular narratives about the Crusades, by contrast, have dramatically shifted to religious and ideological viewpoints. Starting with the American intervention in Iraq in 1991 (The First Gulf War) and culminating in the American (i.e. Western) so called 'War on Terror' campaigns, the Crusades have become synonymous with American/Western interventions in the region. Characterized as 'the neo-Crusades', the general (military and political) American/Western intervention in the region (especially after the Arab Spring) is seen as a religious doctrine for carrying out a Christian mission to subdue, dominate and destroy Islam, both as a religion and as a civilization. Armed with neo-colonial doctrines of American imperial ideology and its divine 'manifest destiny', American conflicts in the Middle East seem, according to those narratives, to be a cosmic struggle between Islam and Christianity. Unlike the official narratives in Jordan, within the context of social media and popular discourse, 'Crusades' and 'neo-Crusades' are widely used to depict all Western forces in Iraq and Syria (including Russian forces). In this regard, the Russian forces have been represented as part of the Christian neo-Crusades. Especially after the Russian Orthodox Church championed and supported Russian military intervention in Syria in the name of protecting Christians in the region.

Literature

Determann, J. 'The Crusades in Arab School Textbooks', *Islam and Christian-Muslim Relations* 19 (2008), pp. 199–214.

Dewkat, F. *Iktaa'iah Ahrk Ala'rdn fi a'sr Alhroub Alsalibiah (The Feudality of Transjordan during the Age of Crusades).* Amman, 2016.

Folda, J. *Crusader Art in the Holy Land, From the Third Crusade to the Fall of Acre.* Cambridge, 2005.

Maalouf, A. *The Crusades through Arab Eyes.* London, 1984.

Sinibaldi, M. *Settlement in Crusader Transjordan (1100–1189). A Historical and Archeological Study.* Cardiff, 2014.

3.3 The idea of crusading is still alive in the West – a view from Russia

Vardan Ėrnestovič Bagdasarjan

Historical conflicts between the West and Russia had, in their essence, the character of the 'Crusades', although they were carried out under various ideological banners. The essence of 'Crusades' in their original sense was determined by the installation of the project which sought to implement Christian rule over the entire world. With the end of the era of the 'Crusades', the colonial expansion of the Western states began, genetically continuing the campaigns of the crusaders. The goal of the expansionist projects initiated in the Western community, which included the 'Third Reich', was to create a world empire. These projects differed in forms but had a common essence: world political domination. This allows for interpreting them as being in succession with the expansionism of the 'crusaders'.

Russia was objectively the main obstacle to the implementation of the projects of world political domination. Moreover, it presented an alternative to the world in regard to the projects of world empire-building put forward by the West. In accordance with this role, Russia became the main target of the neo-crusader forces.

In recent years, the notion of a coming era of new religious wars has been actively introduced into our social consciousness. The impression of a return to the Middle Ages is being formed: the creation of Caliphates, the rise of new Crusades, the execution of non-believers and heretics. A viewpoint is spreading that religions inevitably produce religious conflict in the form of the fundamental confrontation between the devout and non-believers. According to Samuel P. Huntington (1993), modern Western civilization is not based on religion, but on the first secular societal foundation of history. Secularism has become, in this way, the advised practice to free humanity from the impasse of continual religious confrontation.

On the level of Western political elites, the idea of being in succession from the crusaders remains. For instance, Ronald Reagan talked about the 'Crusade' against communism, and George W. Bush spoke of a 'Crusade against terrorism' – rhetoric that was often repeated.[1] During the time of the 'Crusades', the West entered a track of civilization expansion and got stuck in it. The track of the 'Crusades' still forms the logic for world confrontation. Today, overcoming the historical track of the 'Crusades' remains the primary exhortation to the West from the standpoint of the collective security of all mankind.

The images of the new religious war – terrorist attacks, broadcasted executions of heretics and destroyed cultural heritage – have already shaken the consciousness of humanity. But under the banner of a fight against religious fundamentalism, a veritable de-Christianization and de-Islamization will take place. The result will be, in lieu of a supposed religious totalitarianism, an absolute secular totalitarianism.

The fact that the context of Islamic culture was specifically chosen for the formation of a war zone is entirely logical. The 'Muslim factor', or the unique utility of the region for the purposes of a large-scale war, is the geographical position of Islamic countries.[2] This position can be characterized as central among Old World civilizations. The traditional domain of Islam borders zones of Western Christianity, the Eastern Orthodox Church and other religions.[3] The theatre of war, should it take place, would engulf virtually the entire Old World. The North American continent would, once again, find itself removed from the primary field of conflict.

As a matter of fact, the bloodiest wars in human history arose on the platform of secular culture. Accordingly, the cause of war cannot be attributed to religious differences.

There are, indeed, positive instances of religious coexistence. In particular, the history of Russian civilization demonstrates inter-religious complementarity. All three religions identified by religious scholars as belonging to the religious groups of Christianity (in its Eastern Orthodox branch), Islam and Tibetan Buddhism are traditional Russian confessions. In contrast to Europe, and in spite of its religious diversity, Russia did not participate in religious warfare. Hence, the origin of conflict is not found in religious differences, but in the system in which the respective religions are located.

So what exactly is religious extremism: Jihadism, or the new 'Crusades'? It is important to establish that religious extremism is sharply at odds with traditional religions. A religious outer shell is employed, while the core could be defined as a variant of fascist ideology revived under the guise of religion.

Each religion has made its contribution to the spiritual development of mankind, and competition between religions (if such a concept is even appropriate) is competition in the fulfilment of good deeds. Indeed, the provocation of religious wars may be identified as not only an anti-religious project, but also as a project of global political domination by a third, non-religious force.

Literature

Сатановский Е. Я. Россия и Ближний Восток. Котел с неприятностями. М., 2012 (Satanovsky E. Ya. *Russia and Middle East. A Copper with Troubles*. Moskow, 2012).

Соловьев В.С. Три разговора о войне, прогрессе и конце всемирной истории. М., 2015 (Solovyov V.S. *Three Conversations on War, Progress and the End of World History*. Moskow, 2015).

Сулакшин С.С., Багдасарян В.Э., Балмасов С.С. и др. Россия и мир. Российский мировой проект. / Под общей редакцией С.С. Сулакшина. в 2-х томах, М., 2016. (Sulakshin S.S., Bagdasaryan V. E., Balmasov S.S., etc. *Russia and World. Russian World Project*, under general edition of S. S. Sulakshin. 2 volumes, Moskow, 2016).

Эль Мюрид (Несмиян А.). ИГИЛ. «Исламское государство» и Россия. Столкновение неизбежно? М., 2016. (El Myurid (Nesmiyan A.). ISIL. '*The Islamic state' and Russia*. Collision is inevitable? Moskow, 2016).

3.4 Still a particular interest in the former 'Outremer' – a (first) view from France

Michel Balard

[The editors would like to thank Fabien Bastian and Dr. Miriam Sénécheau for their valuable help with the translation.]

In France, research on the Crusades reaches back centuries. It has been characterized by a manifold of differing trends in the course of time. Interest in the subject is unquestionably made clear in the considerable participation by Northern and Southern Frenchmen in crusading expeditions, particularly the County of Toulouse. Jacques Bongars (1554–1612) had already identified this in the 17th century. He highlighted the roles of the French in the Crusades in his book, *Gesta Dei per Francos* (Hannover, 1611). To this day, two memorial sites are especially meaningful for the history of the Crusades. The first is Vézelay, where Bernard of Clairvaux preached his Easter sermon; the second is Aigues-Mortes, the harbour Louis IX (Saint Louis) used as the starting point for his expeditions.

It was at the beginning of the 19th century that the first complete overview of the Crusades was published, written by Joseph Michaud. His works on the Crusades consisted of a seven-volume *Histoire des croisades* (History of the Crusades, 1812–1822) alongside the *Bibliothèque des croisades* (Library of the Crusades, 1829), a four-volume compilation of sources. His work provided a well-documented history of events that inflated the heroism of each crusader who set out to conquer and civilize Asia. Michaud wrote precisely at the time the French announced the conquest of Algeria. Michaud's work can be regarded as a glorification of the colonial expansion of France. The great migration of Christian peoples would have, according to the author, contributed to the withering away of 'Islamism' and to the 'fall of the Kingdom of the Koran'.

The work of Paul Riant (1836–1898) appeared at the end of the 19th century. Riant had founded the *Société de l'Orient latin* in 1875. He continued the publication of the *Recueil des Historiens des Croisades* under the auspices of the *Académie des Inscriptions et Belles-Lettres*. Additionally, he financially supported the *Archives de l'Orient latin* as well as the *Revue de l'Orient latin*. The forgotten work of Charles-Martial Allemand-Lavigerie should also be mentioned in this context.

Research on the Crusades in the first half of the 20th century was characterized by the masterful and complete overview by René Grousset (1885–1952). His work is based on a deep knowledge of both

Western and Eastern sources. It provides a very lively telling of the Crusades and a very precise description of the institutions overseas, although the accomplishments of the Franks through colonialism are strongly emphasized. Contemporaneous to Grousset was the book *La chrétienté et l'idée de croisade* (in two volumes, 1954–1956). It was started by Paul Alphandéry (1875–1932) and continued by Alphonse Dupront (1905–1990). Dupront expanded the scope of this research with the publication of his *De croisade* (in four volumes), wherein he investigates the consistency and changes of this myth in the collective unconscious throughout time. Dupront points out that at least until the beginning of the 19th century, there was a ubiquitous societal yearning towards the holy sites in Syria and Palestine. This was seen as a striving towards the sacred, as a spiritual adventure. This nourished one of the most consequential sources of the development of modern Europe.

While contemporary historiography of the Crusades (particularly Anglo-Saxon historians) tends to separate the history of the expeditions from the history of the nations founded by the Franks, French research connects these two aspects. The *Histoire des croisades* by Jean Richard (1995) serves as an example of this. In his excellent and complete overview, Richard merges the research of the idea and institutions of the Crusades – the research of the different crusader 'waves' and the Frankish society in the 'new overseas fatherland'. Michel Balard utilizes the same approach in his books, *Croisades et Orient latin* (2001) and *Latins en Orient XIe–XVe siècle* (2006). Balard's main focus is on the participants of the Italian maritime republics in the Crusades and on the establishment of trading enterprises in the nations conquered by the crusaders.

Apart from these general works on the Crusades, French research either focused on the regions conquered by the crusaders or on special subject matter. Some aspects that were studies specifically were the Principality of Antioch (Claude Cahen), the County of Tripoli (Jean Richard), the County of Edessa (Monique Amouroux-Mourad), Frankish Morea (Antoine Bon) and the Latin Kingdom of Jerusalem (Jean Richard, Elisabeth Crouzet-Pavan). Several excellent publications came from the biographies of some of the most important figures of the Crusades: Peter the Hermit (Jean Flori), Bohemund of Antioch (Jean Flori), Raynald of Châtillon (Pierre Aubé), Richard the Lionheart (Jean Flori). Flori is to thank for the analysis of the concepts of the holy wars and the modalities of the sermon. Martin Aurell, contrarily, dealt with the critique of the Crusades by its contemporaries. These are examples of the rich and varied French historiography of the

Crusades. Paul Deschamps masterfully researched the crusader castles in the Holy Land, while the orders of chivalry, the Templars, the Hospitallers and the Order of the Teutonic Knights have all been the object of in-depth research (Alain Demurger, Pierre-Vincent Claverie, Sylvain Gouguenheim). An international study of the late Crusades, under the supervision of Daniel Baloup, culminated in a five-volume publication. Jacques Paviot researched undertakings of the Crusades in the 14th and 15th centuries. And might one still be able to say that the Latin states in Syria and Palestine can be equated to precursors of French colonialism? To hold to this assertion would mean to forget that these states were populated by people of various Western origins. Certainly, people from France participated in the Crusades, but also people of Italian, German and Catalonian descents, among others.

A summary of French research on the period of the Crusades is as follows: increasing research in the Mediterranean region and a host of source editions but only a few studies on the Northern Crusades. The Northern Crusades are dealt with in the work of Charles Higounet, *Les Allemands en Europe centrale et orientale au Moyen Age* (1989). In this work, he researched the conflict between Germans and Slavs, the contact between both cultural groups and the respective reactions to these developments. One should not forget the expeditions against the Cathars in Southern France, which were researched by Monique Zerner and Jean-Louis Biget. They are still understood as a form of aggression of the Northern French on the people of Southern France.

Today in France, the concept of a Crusade has become very strained. At times, it is used to designate large collective endeavours, e.g. in matters of public health. Contrarily, it is also used polemically by one portion of society, namely, as a way to characterize Western and Israeli politics in the Middle East. This is undoubtedly a mistake as there are no similarities between the ideology of the crusaders – who set off for the Holy Land to search for their salvation – and that of the Israelis, who primarily endeavour to settle in the land of their ancestors from the times of antiquity.

Literature

Alphandéry, P. Dupront, A. *La chrétienté et l'idée de croisade (Christendom and the Idea of Crusading)*, rééd. avec une postface de M. Balard, éd. Albin Michel. Paris, 1995.

Aurell, M. *Des chrétiens contre les croisades (XIIe–XIIIe siècle) (Christians against the Crusades (12th–13th Centuries))*. Paris, 2013.

Balard, M. «L'historiographie des croisades au XXe siècle (Contribution de la France, de l'Allemagne et de l'Italie)» (The Historiography of the Crusades of the 20th Century (Contributions of France, Germany and Italy) *Revue historique*, t. CCCII/4, 2000, pp. 973–999.

Balard, M. *Les Latins en Orient (XIe-XVe siècle) (The Latin Europeans in the Orient (11th–15th Centuries))*, coll. Nouvelle Clio. Paris, 2006.

Claverie, P-V. *L'ordre du Temple en Terre sainte et à Chypre au XIIIe siècle (The Order of the Temple in the Holy Land and at Cyprus at the 13th Century)*, 3 vols. Nicosie, 2005.

Deschamps, P. *Les Châteaux des croisés en Terre Sainte (The Crusader Castles in the Holy Land)*, 3 vols. Paris, 1934–1973.

Demurger, A. *Les Hospitaliers. De Jérusalem à Rhodes 1050–1317 (The Knights Hospitaller. From Jerusalem to Rhodes 1030–1317)*. Paris, 2013.

Demurger, A. *Les Templiers. Une chevalerie chrétienne au Moyen Age (The Templar Knights. A Christian Chivalry of the Middle Ages)*. Paris, 2005.

Dupront, A. *Du sacré: croisades et pèlerinages, images et langages (About the Sacred: Crusades and Pilgrimages, Image and Language)*. Paris, 1987.

Flori, J. *La guerre sainte. La formation de l'idée de croisade dans l'Occident chrétien (The Holy War. The Development of the Idea of Crusading in the Latin World)*. Paris, 2001.

Flori, J. *Prêcher la croisade (XIe-XIIIe siècle). Communication et propaganda (Preaching the Crusade (11th–13th Centuries). Communication and Propaganda)*. Paris, 2012.

Grousset, R. *Histoire des croisades et du royaume franc de Jérusalem (History of the Crusades and of the Frankish Kingdom of Jerusalem)*, 3 vols. Paris, 1934–1936.

Michaud, J. *Histoire des croisades (History of the Crusades)*, 7 vols. Paris, 1812–1822.

Paviot, J. *Les ducs de Bourgogne, la croisade et l'Orient (fin XIVe–XVe siècle) (The Dukes of Burgundy, the Crusade and the Orient (End of 14th–15th Centuries))*. Paris, 2003.

Richard, J. *Histoire des croisades (History of the Crusades)*. Paris, 1995.

3.5 The 'Island of the Knights' on the fault line to the Islamic world – a view from Malta

Emanuel Buttigieg

During the years of the First Crusade (1095–1099) to Jerusalem, the Maltese Islands were in an ambivalent position. Decades prior to this, Norman Christian warriors were already conquering the fractious eclectic states of southern Italy. In 1060–61, the brothers Robert Guiscard (c.1015–1085) and Roger (c.1031–1101) conquered Messina in Sicily, which was to act as the springboard of the thirty-year Norman conquest of Muslim Sicily. In 1091, Roger attacked Malta, whose population at this point was largely Muslim. The Muslim communities in Malta were subjected to overlordship, but life continued largely unchanged. It would take centuries for Maltese culture to shift from an Arabic-Muslim one to a Latin Christian one, although the modern Maltese language is a living reminder of that Arabic phase. Muslim Malta as a historical fact is vehemently denied in Maltese popular imagination, which clings to the notion of a Christian community liberated by Christian Normans. Like Spain[4] and Sicily,[5] Malta was one of the places that the Crusades permanently returned to Christendom, unlike the fleeting conquests in the Middle East. Maltese historians have rarely presented this part of Malta's story as a chapter of the Crusades, and it is not remembered as such in popular memory.

The perception of the Crusades and their connection with Malta is forged by the 268 years (1530–1798) during which the islands were the headquarters of the military-religious Order of St. John the Baptist (the Hospitallers). Some chronologies actually place the end of the Crusades in June 1798, when the forces of Revolutionary-Republican France under Napoleon ousted the Hospitallers from Malta.[6] It does not matter that – technically speaking – the Hospitallers were not crusaders; the lure of the Christian knight in shining armour fighting Muslims still captivates. Hospitaller Malta was engaged in one long Crusade at sea against Islam, and this dimension has remained ingrained in the popular imagination. It is also a powerful element in the promotion of Malta as a tourist destination: Malta *is* 'the Island of the Knights'. The eight-pointed Hospitaller Cross has unequivocally become 'the Maltese Cross'. Some would even like to see the George Cross (awarded to Malta by Great Britain during the Second World War), which appears on Malta's flag, replaced by the Maltese Cross.

The defining moment in the relationship between the Hospitallers and Malta was the Ottoman Siege during the summer of 1565[7] – 'the

Great Siege', often described as the last battle of the Crusades. As with all historical events, myths arose around the 1565 siege and its protagonist, Grand Master Jean de (la) Valette (r.1557–1658). Hence, the traditional view of the siege – held by Maltese historians and the wider public alike – is that 1565 was one of (if not *the*) last great struggles of the Crusades, and that by repulsing the Ottomans, the Hospitallers and Maltese saved Europe.

By contrast, in recent years, a more discerning view of 1565 has been espoused by some Maltese historians, one that is not interested in whether this was a 'good' or 'bad' event, but which instead sees it as part of the wider rhythms of the Mediterranean. What was at stake in 1565 was not Europe or Christendom, but the survival of the Order of St. John as an institution. Both views of 1565, and by extension the Crusades, coexist side-by-side, neither seeming poised to overwhelm the other. Similarly, perceptions of Grand Master Valette have fluctuated over the centuries. A statue of him in Valletta was only inaugurated on the 21st of November 2012, arguably because the city itself had stood as a monument to its founder for centuries.

The year 2015 marked the 450th anniversary of the Great Siege. This generated a whole spate of exhibitions, books and TV programmes. The 450th anniversary came on the heels of 2014, a year of national political anniversaries marking 50 years of Independence (21st of September 1964), 40 years of Malta becoming a Republic (13th of December 1974), 35 years since the closure of the British naval base (31st of March 1979) and 10 years of European Union Membership (1st of May 2004). It also coincided with a social media environment in which discourses about 'Crusades' are often coming up in the wake of the migration crisis in the Mediterranean and the activities of Islamic fundamentalists. Linguistically, to wage a Crusade (*kruċjata* in Maltese) is generally used in a positive sense, for example, a Crusade in defence of the environment.

Malta finds itself once again on the fault line of a sensitive physical–cultural frontier, which creates both certainty and anxiety. An academically informed historical approach to the past acknowledges its complexity, whereas memory tends to simplify and be selective; yet, these two are constantly interacting with each other. It is in the interstice of this interaction that Maltese perspectives of the Crusades, as well as crusading perceptions of Malta, are formed. The challenge is how to ensure that an inclusive narrative that preserves local character, while being open to the world, prevails over one that favours an introverted building of walls.

Literature

Buttigieg, E. *Nobility, Faith and Masculinity. The Hospitaller Knights of Malta.* London, 2011.
Camilleri, M. (ed.) *Besieged. Malta 1565.* Malta, 2015.
Dalli, C. *Malta. The Medieval Millenium.* Malta, 2006.
Mallia-Milanes, V. 'The Siege of Malta, 1565, Revisited', *Storja* 2015, pp. 1–18.
Spiteri, S. *The Great Siege: Knights vs Turks.* Malta, 2005.

Selected popular items:

Age of Empires III. (2005). [computer game].
Balbi di Correggio, Francisco, *The Siege of Malta 1565*, translated by E. Bradford. London, 2003.
Ball, David. *The Sword and the Scimitar.* London, 2004.
Willocks, Tim. *The Religion.* London, 2006.

3.6 Crusades and maritime expansion – a view from Portugal

Paula Maria de Carvalho Pinto Costa

In 1095, following the Council of Clermont, a synthesis between two important elements emerged: pilgrimage and holy war. This was emblematic of the new spirituality of that time. From that moment onwards, in Portugal, the Crusades were gradually associated with reconquest. The study of the Crusades is close to the study of the Religious and Military Orders, which became one of the most systematic specialities of the Portuguese historiography since the 1980s.

In terms of the articulation of the reconquest and the Crusades, Pope Paschal II (1099–1118) contributed greatly when he equated the struggle on the Iberia to the one that took place in the Holy Land.[8] In this sense, the same privileges were granted to people who participated in these different situations. Santiago de Compostela became a place of pilgrimage, sharing equal status with Jerusalem and Rome.

There are still doubts concerning the oldest document in Portugal that clearly references the Crusades. Some authors highlight the bull in 1179, the *Manifestus probatum est* granted by Pope Alexander III, which offered the kingdom his protection and recognized its independence. Nevertheless, in this context, it is possible to include the Siege of Lisbon, which expelled the Muslims in 1147. During this military campaign, some northern knights, on their way to the Second Crusade, helped the Portuguese king.

Dias Dinis, a Portuguese priest and historian dedicated to the history of missions and discoveries, distinguished three different types of papal documents: letters of encouragement promoting the Portuguese reconquest (1179–1234); Crusade letters of spiritual support (indulgences) given to Portuguese who fought in the Holy Land or subsidized those actions (1234–1341) and Crusade letters against the Muslims of Granada and Morocco, by granting some ecclesiastical income to the realm (1341–1411).

In fact, the foundation bull of the Order of Christ by John XXII (1319) is paradigmatic. It opens a new phase – it is *an authentic bull of permanent Crusade against Islamites*. The Order of Christ represented the continuity of the concept of Crusade and supported the maritime policy of the crown. In 1341, after the battle of Salado (1340) where Christian and Muslim armies engaged in combat, Pope Benedict XII gave a tenth of ecclesiastical revenue in the realm to Portuguese king Afonso IV in support of the Crusade against Morocco and Granada.

This link between crusading and the objectives of the monarch reinforced the overseas expansion in Morocco and the Atlantic. The conquest of Ceuta (1415) in Africa was a more symbolic movement. From this moment onwards, crusading became a recurrent theme in Portugal. On the one hand, kings charged the church property to obtained funds, and, on the other hand, the indulgences stimulated the participation of people in those actions.

In medieval Portugal, the ideological concept of Crusade was applied outside the scope of Muslims. For example, the King João II (1481) asked the Pope for a full indulgence for those who died in the exploration of the Gulf of Guinea and the South Atlantic. In consequence, the concept of Crusade was related to a strong messianic dimension, particularly with King D. Manuel (1495–1521). He wanted to recover Jerusalem, an ambition related to the desire for control of the Mediterranean, enhanced by Turkish advances towards the West. Although this utopia was outgrown, the ideal of Crusade did not disappear completely from Portuguese history. For instance, Gil Vicente, considered the chief dramatist in the 16th century, wrote the *Auto da Barca do Inferno.* In this text, the author, satirizing Portuguese society, condemned to hell several characters and, in contrast, saved four crusaders knights because they were useful. Indeed, the ideal of Crusade was transformed and adapted to the expansion towards Brazil and the Far East. Furthermore, it was used as a way to support colonization and Christianization.

In contemporary times, in Portugal, the Crusades are regarded as a topic of study and an area of research, blended with research about the military orders. The ideal of Crusade, as such, no longer exists, and it does not have any institutional dimensions. In Portugal, the religious orders, including the military ones, were disbanded in the 1830s. Nowadays, the Military Orders are honorary orders, aggregated to the Presidency of the Republic and are used by the Portuguese State to distinguish citizens.

Literature

Flori, J. 'Croisade' (Crusade). In *Prier et combattre. Dictionnaire Critique des Ordres Militaires Européens au Moyen Âge (Pray and fight. Critical Dictionary of European Military Orders in the Middle Ages).* coord. Nicole Bériou e Philippe Josserand. Éditions Fayard, 2009, pp. 276–278.

Fonseca, Luís Adão da. *O Condestável D. Pedro de Portugal (The Constable Don Pedro of Portugal).* Porto, 1982.

Fonseca, Luís Adão da, Maria Cristina Pimenta, Paula Pinto Costa. 'The Papacy and the Crusades in XVth Century Portugal'. In *La Papauté et les Croisades (The Papacy and the Crusades)*, ed. Michel Balard. Proceedings of the Society of the Study of the Crusades and the Latin East. Crusades – Subsidia, 3. Ashgate, 2011, pp. 141–154.

Oliveira, Luís Filipe, Luís Adão da Fonseca, Maria Cristina Pimenta, Paula Pinto Costa. 'The Military Orders. In *The Historiography of Medieval Portugal, c. 1950–c.2010: A Collective Book and a Collaborative Project*, ed. José Mattoso, Maria de Lurdes Rosa, Bernardo Vasconcelos e Sousa, Maria João Branco. Lisboa, 2011, pp. 425–457.

Thomaz, Luís Filipe. 'Cruzada' (Crusade). In *Dicionário de História Religiosa de Portugal (Dictionary of the Religious History of Portugal)*, dir. Carlos Moreira Azevedo, volume C-I. Lisbon, 2000, pp. 31–38.

3.7 The Crusades confront the orthodox – a Greek Cypriot viewpoint

Nicholas Coureas

According to the typical narratives of Greek Cypriot historians, in general the Crusades brought radical religious, economic and institutional changes to Cyprus. The result of the Third Crusade was the conquest of Cyprus in the summer of 1191 and the establishment of the French Roman Catholic dynasty – the Lusignan dynasty (1192–1474) that went on to rule the island for nearly three hundred years – is included in these narratives. However, the changes that occurred are viewed negatively, especially due to the fact that the indigenous Greek Church of Cyprus had to acknowledge papal primacy. The Greek word for Crusade, *staurophoria*, which literally means 'bearing the cross', is semantically neutral. Nevertheless, the conquest of Cyprus during the Third Crusade – and of Constantinople during the Fourth – makes most Greek Cypriots historically associate this word with the conquest of Greek lands.

Today, the Latin or Roman Catholic Church in Cyprus is a minority church, like its Armenian, Anglican and Maronite counterparts. Currently, there is no confrontation between Christian denominations on the island. During the period of the Crusades, the reality was different. Greek Cypriot historians emphasized the conflict between the Latin and Greek churches. The late Theodore Papadopoullos, editor of a multi-volume History of Cyprus written in the Greek language, considered the establishment of the Latin Church in Cyprus in 1196 – following the island's conquest – as being a means of enforcing the complete subordination of the native Greek majority population to the new Latin ruling class. They attempted this by ensuring religious subordination, not simply by political and social subjection. He also believed that the frontier role of Cyprus, which formed a geographical border in the struggle between Byzantium and Islam, transformed itself into a social frontier following the conquest of the island by the Latins in the Third Crusade. This transformation took place through the implantation of the Western feudal system, which changed the ruling class from Byzantine Greek to French. Additionally, the legal system was changed by implementing Western legal practices and legal institutions – the so-called Assizes and the High and Burgess Courts – even if they had Byzantine influences. Nevertheless, Papadopoullos had two reasons for considering the long-term influence of Western political, legal, religious and social institutions on the Greeks of

Cyprus to have been only transitory. Firstly, at the time of conquest in 1191, the Crusades had lost their initial impetus. Secondly, with the discovery of America in 1492, the Eastern Mediterranean, including Cyprus, steadily lost its importance to the West. Therefore, Papadopoullos stated that with the Ottoman Conquest of 1570, Cyprus became as Greek as it had been in 1192. He said nothing about the Syrians, Armenians, Copts and other Eastern Christians then living in Cyprus. He saw the Lusignan and Venetian periods (1191–1570) as one of confrontation between the incoming Latins and the native Greeks, despite the literary efflorescence of the period. Some of these literary developments include historical chronicles and poetry written in Old French, Latin, Greek and Italian. Another development was iconography interacting with Greek, Italian and Syrian artistic styles. Furthermore, there was the enrichment of the Greek dialect of Cyprus with French, Italian and Catalan words that all continue to shape Cypriot culture to this day.

Aikaterini Aristeidou, in her article about the consequences of the Crusades on the economic development of Lusignan Cyprus, states that while the Crusades took place with papal approval for primarily religious reasons, 'they assumed the character of extended raids in which many adventurers, nobles down on their luck and people seeking to gain from plunder took part'. For her, the Third Crusade, which led to the conquest of Cyprus, had the greatest impact. Politically, it resulted in the island becoming a Western kingdom detached from Byzantium. In present-day Greek Cypriot historiography, it is perceived as a Medieval Greek Empire of the Christian Orthodox faith to which Cyprus naturally belonged, having developed close relations with the Latin kingdom of Jerusalem. In religion, it led to the establishment of the Latin Church and its regular orders: monks, friars and the military orders of the Templars and Hospitallers, as well as the subordination of the indigenous Orthodox Church to the papacy. These religious developments are interpreted in a negative light. Aristeidou particularly stresses the development of trade in Cyprus that resulted from the crusader conquest. Cypriot agricultural products (sugar, olive oil, wine and cereals) were exported to Western Europe. Spices and various clothes, silks and other textiles traversed westwards, not only from Cyprus but also from Eastern lands via Cyprus. The Venetians, Genoese, Pisans and merchants of Marseilles played an important role in carrying out trade and obtaining privileges on Cyprus. But according to Aristeidou, only the Latin nobles and merchants profited from the wealth brought about by the development of trade, not the indigenous Greek population.

In popular culture, the one Lusignan king who is important in Cypriot folk lore is Peter I (1359–1369), whose extra-marital affair with Joan d'Aleman formed the basis of the traditional Cypriot ballad titled, 'Arodaphnousa'. His reign was also featured in a popular television series some years ago, with an emphasis on his extra-marital affairs. This, however, is an isolated example. And it should be stressed here that the word 'Crusade' has a plethora of popular associations in Western cultures but not in Greek Cypriot culture, since it is not a concept that forms part of its traditions.

Literature

Aristeidou, Aik. 'Hoi epiptoseis ton Staurophorion sten oikonomike anaptyxe tes Kyprou' (The Effects of the Crusades on the Economic Development of Cyprus). In *Cyprus and the Crusades*, ed. N. Coureas and J. Riley Smith, Nicosia, 1995, pp. 355–364.

Papadopoullos, Th. 'Dome kai Leitourgeia tou Feoudarkhikou Politeumatos', in *Historia tes Kyprou*, IV, *Mesaionikon Basileion, Henetokratia* ('The Structure and Function of the Feudal State', in *History of Cyprus*, 4 (1995), *The Medieval Kingdom, Venetian Rule*), ed. *idem*, Nicosia, 1995, pp. 543–665.

Papadopoullos, Th. 'Dome kai Proeleuse tes taxeos ton Eugenon', in *Historia tes Kyprou*, IV, *Mesaionikon Basileion, Henetokratia* ('The Structure and Origins of the Nobility', in *History of Cyprus*, vol. 4, *The Medieval Kingdom, Venetian Rule*), ed. *idem*, Nicosia, 1995, pp. 759–784.

Papadopoullos, Th. 'He ekklesia Kyprou kata ten Periodo tes Frangokratias', in *Historia tes Kyprou, IV, Mesaionikon Basileion, Henetokratia* ('The Church of Cyprus during the Period of Frankish Rule', in *History of Cyprus, vol. 4, The Medieval Kingdom, Venetian Rule*), ed. *idem*, Nicosia, 1995, pp. 785–841.

3.8 Western aggression and Greco-Latin interaction – a view from Greece

Nikolaos G. Chrissis

In Modern Greek historiography, the Crusades (*σταυροφορίες* – literally 'bearing of the cross') have hardly been examined on their own merits, but rather as an adjunct to the history of Byzantium (traditionally seen as the 'medieval Greek Empire') and the Greek lands.

Greek historians have mostly dealt with crusading and its repercussions in two contexts:

1 The first is as an episode of the Byzantine Empire's relations with Latin powers. The crusaders generally make an appearance when their armies approach the lands of the empire, and more or less fade out of sight after they have moved farther east or south. The incident that stands out most of all is the conquest of Constantinople by the Fourth Crusade in 1204.

Since the dawn of modern Greek historiography, the Crusades have been inscribed in the wider commercial, political and military infiltration of Westerners within the Byzantine sphere, alongside phenomena such as the activities of Italian maritime powers (especially Venice) in the area, the Norman threat to the empire and the relations between the Greek and the Roman Churches. All these topics have been explored in greater detail in Greek historiography than the crusading aspect of the Western involvement in the East. One exception is the examination of Byzantine perceptions of the crusade and holy war, particularly by Athina Kolia-Dermitzaki.

Overall, the Crusades are seen as an incipient form of Western European colonialism. Motivation for crusading is presented as a mixture of religious fervour and material concerns. References to crusading activity in other fronts outside the Holy Land are rare. The later Crusades are also absent for the most part. Accounts usually end with the fall of Acre in 1291, with the exception of campaigns against the Turks in the 14th and 15th centuries as they had a direct bearing on Byzantium.

2 Outside Byzantine history 'proper', most of the attention on the western presence in the area has focused on the Latin dominions established as a result of the Fourth Crusade (1204), namely, the short-lived Latin Empire of Constantinople,[9] the kingdom of Thessalonica, the more durable principality of Achaia, the duchy of Athens and Thebes as well as the Venetian and other Italian-held islands and coastal possessions,[10] some of which survived up to the modern era.

In terms of contemporary relevance, the Crusades, they do not have a far-reaching resonance in modern Greece. In school textbooks, they are presented as significant events with long-lasting consequences for the relations between Western Europe and the Muslim world. But they are regarded as hardly touching the 'core' of Greek national history, which is perceived as distinct from both sides. A significant exception, however, is the Fourth Crusade as it is seen as a major turning point. Indeed, the interpretation of Byzantine-Latin interaction often gets entangled in the question of the place of modern Greece in the world, particularly in Europe.

Throughout the 19th and in the first half of the 20th century, Western activities in Byzantine territories were seen in primarily two different lights. First, these Western activities were viewed from the perspective of Greek national history in the aftermath of the War of Independence and the establishment of the modern Greek state. Secondly, they were seen from the perspective of confessional historiography focusing on the relations between the Orthodox and Catholic Churches. Both approaches were generally hostile to the 'foreign' presence and intervention in Greek lands. In the dominant interpretative schema of Greek history, that is, of the continuity of Hellenism through the ages, the period from 1204/1453 to the 19th century is perceived and described as 'Hellenism under Foreign Domination'. This includes the domination by both Turks and Latins. The 'father' of modern Greek historiography, Konstantinos Paparrigopoulos (1815–1891), was very influential in formulating this view. He considered the Fourth Crusade as part of a long-standing Western aggression towards Byzantium/Greece, a view shared by most of his contemporaries. Historical novels and theatrical plays set in Latin-held Greece that promoted patriotic messages of national liberation against foreign oppressors were in vogue during that period (e.g. Dimitrios Bernardakis, *Maria Doxapatri*, 1858; Alexandros Papadiamantis, *Oi Emporoi ton Ethnon*, 1882–1883).

Research in the late 20th and early 21st centuries no longer regards the relationship between Greeks and Latins as a solely antagonistic one, examining in greater detail the realities of intercultural contacts, social organization as well as mutual influences in art, literature, religious practices, etc. This is particularly the case in the Peloponnese and the islands, where Latin presence proved more enduring and cooperation between the two sides was motivated by the Turkish threat.[11] In recent works, there has been a greater emphasis on the osmosis of Greek and Latin elements in local societies, which is reflected also in a shift of terminology (e.g. 'History of the Greco-Latin East').

It is significant that the period of this change has coincided with the opening up of Greek scholarship to the international academic community, the participation of Greece in the EEC/EU and the renewed discussion regarding the role of modern Greece in Europe, touching on crucial issues of national identity and historical memory.

Literature

Dourou-Eliopoulou, M. *Από τη δυτική Ευρώπη στην ανατολική Μεσόγειο: Οι σταυροφορικές ηγεμονίες στη Ρωμανία (13ος–15ος αιώνας) (From Western Europe to the Eastern Mediterranean: The crusading lordships in Romania (13th–15th c.))*. Athens, 2012.

Giannakopoulos, D. *Εικόνες του δυτικοευρωπαίου μέσα από την ιστορία. Επιστημονική επεξεργασία και αναπαράσταση της Λατινοκρατίας στην Ελλάδα του 19ου αι. (The Image of the Western European through History: Scholarly Examination and Representation of the Period of Latin Rule in 19th-Century Greece)*. Athens, 2013.

Kolia-Dermitzaki, A., *Συνάντηση Ανατολής και Δύσης στα εδάφη της αυτοκρατορίας: Οι απόψεις των Βυζαντινών για τους σταυροφόρους (Meeting of East and West in the Lands of the Empire: Byzantine Views of the Crusaders)*. Athens, 1994.

Papadia-Lala, A., 'La venetocrazia nel pensiero greco. Storicità, realtà, prospettive' (The Venetocracy in Greek thought. Historicity, Reality, Perspectives), in *Italia-Grecia: temi e storiografie a confronto (Italy-Greece: Themes and Historiographies in Comparison)*, eds. Ch. Maltezou and G. Ortalli. Venice, 2001, pp. 61–70.

Paparrigopoulos, K., *Ιστορία του Ελληνικού Έθνους (History of the Greek Nation)*, esp. vols. 4–5. Athens, 1886–87; 2nd ed.

Selected popular items:

Bernardakis, D. *Μαρία Δοξαπατρή (Maria Doxapatri)*, 1857.

Papadiamantis, A. *Οι Έμποροι των Εθνών (The Merchants of Nations)*. s.l., 1882–1883.

3.9 The former victors over the Crusades in Palestine – a view from Egypt

Taef Kamal El-Azhari

Al-Hurub Al-Salibyya – Arabic for 'wars of the cross' – is a concept that occupies and dominates the most important notion that the education system seeks to impart to students of all ages and at every level. Although the Crusades only lasted two centuries, they have a greater status in shaping the core of Egyptian identity than the vast and distinguished pharaonic history. At different stages of their schooling, as well as at the university, Egyptian students study how Jerusalem was taken from them by the First Crusade in 1099, and how, during the Fatimid dynasty, the Syrian–Palestinian coastal cities were one by one seized from Egypt by the crusaders. Because the Muslim Kurdish leader, Saladin, founded his dynasty in Cairo, choosing Egypt as the base for his empire in the Middle East, some elevate him to the status as a saint or epic hero, especially after he conquered Jerusalem in 1187 with half of his army being mobilized from Egypt. The Egyptian educational system views Egyptian locals who made major sacrifices with pride – Muslim and Christians alike. Importantly, two out of the seven major Crusades were directed towards Egypt. They occupied part of the Eastern Nile delta in 1218 and in 1248. Under the Mamluk dynasty which succeeded the Ayybids in Egypt and the Middle East in 1250, one sees a major contribution made by different Mamluk kings of Egypt against the crusaders in Syria. King Baibars invaded and seized the crusader principality of Antioch in 1268, while his successor Qalawun seized the final principality of Tripoli in 1289. Khalil, son of Qalawun, who ended the Crusades by seizing Acre in 1291, was so zealous for jihad to the extent that he shipped the dismantled main gate of the crusader cathedral in Acre all the way to Cairo, where his brother reused it as part of his mosque in Medieval Cairo that exists to the present.

This type of history was not only glorified in schools and universities, but was also echoed throughout other media and the arts. They continued to recall the deeds of Saladin.

In the last few decades, with the rise of Muslim fundamentalism, Saladin's legacy receives continued idolization and is recalled for the political purpose of jihad. They seek to gather supporters and followers and create armed militia, like the 'Ansar bait al-Maqdis' or 'Supporters of Jerusalem', the anti-state terrorist organization in Sinai today. This is not only to attack the Israeli state, but also to attack any other Muslims who do not believe in their dogma. They even use the term 'crusaders' for anyone who does not support them, Muslim and Copts alike. These groups have alliances that cross borders with other groups in Iraq and Syria, creating a new challenge for the 21st century.

Literature

Gabrieli, F. *Arab Historians of the Crusades. Selected and Translated from the Arabic Sources by Francesco Gabrieli*, translated from Italian by E.J. Costello. (Islamic World). Berkeley/Los Angeles, 1969.

Hillenbrand, Carole. *The Crusades. Islamic Perspectives.* Edinburgh, 1999.

Hirschler, Konrad. 'The Jerusalem Conquest of 492/1099 in the Medieval Arabic Historiography of the Crusades: From Regional Plurality to Islamic Narrative', in: *Crusades* 13 (2014), pp. 37–76.

Ibn al- Dāwādārī. *Kanz al-durar wa-jāmi' al-ghurar*, vols. 7. *(The Report about the Ayyubid Dynasty)*, ed. by Said abd al-Fattah Asur, Freiburg 1972 and vols. 8 (The Report about the Mamluk Dynasty), ed. by Ulrich Haarmann, Freiburg 1971 (Quellen zur Geschichte des Islamischen Ägyptens, vols. 1h and 1g).

Mallett, A. *Popular Muslim Reactions to the Franks in the Levant, 1097–1291.* New York, 2016.

Sivan, E. *L'Islam et la croisade: idéologie et propaganda dans les reactions muselmans aux croisades (Islam and Crusades: Reactions of Muslims at the Time of the Crusades to Ideology and Propaganda).* Paris, 1968.

3.10 A hostile and aggressive stance of the West towards Turkey based on othering and a double standard – a view from Turkey

Mehmet Ersan

One of the largest and lengthy military actions in history began with the call of Pope Urban II during the Council of Clermont. The participants of this military action were named as 'Franks' by the Muslim historians at the time, while the Ottomans used the concept 'Ehl-i Salîb'. Moreover, today the Turkish use the term 'Haçlılar' for the crusaders. All military actions that began in the 11th century, and were replicated in the following centuries, are described with the term 'Haçlı Seferleri = the Crusades'.

Research on the subject of the Crusades has started to be conducted in Turkey only recently. When one considers the publications on the Crusades, the general view regarding reasons for the Crusades can be compared to the original summons to start crusading in the initial Crusades all the way to the later developments. This will be described in the following part.

After Turkey began to conquer Anatolia in the middle of the 11th century and settle in the area, Byzantium petitioned the Pope for help, being unable to stop the Turkish advances on its own. The Crusades are one of the consequences of this event. The Pope wanted to utilize the Byzantine request for mercenaries to serve at their behest to solve the political, social and economic problems Europe was facing at the time. In order to drive the Turks from Anatolia and conquer the entire Middle East, Pope Urban II gave the summons that started the Crusades. In order to mobilize the masses, he used the slogan, 'liberation of the holy sites and of Eastern Christendom'. Muslims had already conquered Jerusalem in 638 and there had been no attempts to reclaim it from them until the year 1095. The reasons for the Crusades listed in textbooks are summarized as: the holy sites were to be reclaimed from the Muslims; the Pope wanted to bring the church back together; the Byzantines (who could not stop the advances of the Turks) asked the Pope for help; Europe – which found itself in a difficult economic situation – wanted to pick up some of the wealth of the East.

Indeed, the crusader army that departed in 1096 suffered tough losses, but they were able to successfully recapture Jerusalem from the Muslims. However, hundreds of thousands of the crusaders who left to strengthen the Christian presence in the Middle East were wiped out by Sultan Kilij Arslan. Furthermore, subsequent crusader armies who sought to cross Anatolia were unsuccessful and had to take the sea route.

In the years leading up to the conquest of Acre in 1291, the Western world sought to establish itself in the Near East by organizing nine Crusades. They also sought to maintain the land that was conquered and the crusader states that had been established in the region. In contrast, the Turks, along with other Muslim nations, fought to end the Christian presence in the region. Out of these wars arose heroes such as Sultan Kilij Arslan and Mesud I, who attempted to halt the First Crusade in Anatolia. Others were Atabeg Imad ad-Din Zengi, his son Nur ad-Din Zengi and the General of Zengi, who sought to end the presence of the crusaders in Syria and Palestine. And finally there was Saladin, who reclaimed Jerusalem from the crusaders. Both academic texts and school textbooks incorporate the fact that changes in the societal structure occurred as a result of the Crusades (e.g. faith in the church and the clergy decreased; the culture of the East was brought to the West and shaped European development).

Today, in the Turkish public sphere, the prevailing opinion is that the West never lost its interest in the Middle East. Furthermore, the obstacles the Turkish people and Turkey face in international problems – like the wars that are perpetually waged in the region – are a product of the crusader mentality. The outlook, although Latin control of the Middle East was put to an end in 1291, the mentality of the Crusades did not end, still exists. For instance, the endeavours to expel the Turks first out of Europe and then out of Anatolia – in the face of the advances of the Ottoman Empire into the Balkans and Middle Europe – were carried out under the name 'late Crusades'. Additionally, the Treaty of Sèvres, which was to be implemented after the end of the First World War, is viewed as a product of these ideas.

Despite this perception of the Crusades, there is no noteworthy reflection of this in the Turkish film industry, culture or literature. There has not been a film produced or a book written that has impressed the masses, nor has a museum of the Crusades been founded.

In only a few historical films made after the 1970s the crusaders were portrayed primarily as invaders or a military force that went crusading for material gain or to overcome the hunger and privation they were suffering in Europe, which was also a force that drove them not to turn back in the face of fear.

In conclusion, in the Turkish public sphere, the word 'crusader' has a negative connotation. One can even say that in everyday speech, 'Crusade' means 'the perpetually hostile aggressive stance of the West towards Turkey that is based on Othering and a double standard'.

Literature

Altan, E. *Antakya Haçlı Prinkepsliği Tarihi (History of the Principality of Antioch)*. Istanbul, 2014.

Demirkent, I. *Haçlı Seferleri (The Crusades)*. Istanbul, 2004.

Kanat-Devrim Burçak, C. *Sorularla Haçlı Seferleri (The Crusades – Questions and Answers)*. Istanbul, 2013.

Küçüksipahioğlu, B., *Trablus Haçlı Kontluğu Tarihi (History of the County of Tripoli)*. Istanbul, 2007.

Usta, A. *Çıkarların Gölgesinde Haçlı Seferleri (The Crusades in the Shadow of Interests)*. Istanbul, 2008.

3.11 A Crusader-flag falling from the sky – a view from Denmark

Iben Fonnesberg Schmidt

Pope Urban II's call for a Crusade to the Holy Land in 1095 was shared across Latin Christendom. This call also reached the Danish kingdom, which had been officially Christianized in the 960s. Several Danes joined this expedition; among them were Prince Swen and his wife, Florina of Burgundy, along with members of the Burgundian family. Ideas about meritorious warfare had long existed in north-eastern Europe. Following the success of the First Crusade, some ecclesiastical and secular leaders began applying the ideas and rhetoric of the First Crusade to local warfare against non-Christians. The idea of a Crusade in northern Europe received papal sanction in 1147 when Pope Eugenius III authorized a campaign against the pagan Slavs. This Crusade became part of the Second Crusade and was known as the Wendish Crusade. The Danes took part in the Second Crusade but achieved as little as the majority of the other armies involved in the venture. They also undertook a series of campaigns against the Wends in the following decades, but little is known about the participants' motivations and perceptions of their endeavours. The Danes do not appear to have sought papal sanction for their late 12th-century campaigns. Whether these later campaigns should be perceived as Crusades is still a hotly contested topic among Danish historians.

By the late 12th and early 13th centuries, a new series of Danish, Swedish and German Crusades targeted the non-Christian lands in the easternmost part of the Baltic region. These received papal support and spiritual privileges for the participants were granted. Contemporaneous chronicles, such as the one by Henry of Livonia, suggest that many participants viewed their endeavour as similar to the Crusades in the Holy Land. In 1219, the Danish King Valdemar II conquered parts of northern Estonia and created the duchy of Estonia, which remained under the Danish rule until 1346.[12]

Extant sources show that some Danes – it is not known how many – continued to go on Crusades in the East. Among them was Jens Sunesen (d. c. 1203), brother of the Danish Archbishop, Anders Sunesen. With support from the Danish king, in 1164, the Order of St. John, which played such a prominent role in the Crusades in the Holy Land, established a priory at Antvorskov, which enjoyed royal support for its work in the Danish kingdom for many decades.

Danes thus took part in both Crusades to the Holy Land and the Baltic region. However, Danish crusading activity has not played a major role in the construction of modern Danish identity, although it has made an impact through its association with the Danish flag. According to legend, the flag – often used as a symbol of Danish identity and carries a great value for many Danes – fell from the sky during a battle in Estonia. The story appeared in the early 16th-century writings of two Danish historians, Christiern Pedersen and Peder Olesen, who drew on material that is now lost. They ascribed the event to a battle in 1208, but from the late 16th century, it became associated with the Battle of Lyndanisse (Estonia), which took place on the 15th of June, 1219. As Danish nationalistic ideas flourished, the story of the fallen flag stoked the imagination of late 18th- and 19th-century writers and painters and was depicted in several works. The 15th of June became known as 'Valdemar's Day'. Since 1912, it has become a designated day for flying the Danish flag on government buildings in commemoration of the event.

Modern Danish historians long displayed very little interest in the Danish participation in the Crusades in the Holy Land; indeed, the main scholarly contribution was written by a French historian, Paul Riant (1836–88). The Danish contribution to the Second Crusade and the Danish Crusades in the eastern Baltic region around 1200 received somewhat more attention, in so far as they were included, however briefly, in most general works on Danish history. While some Danish historians, including Johannes Steenstrup (1844–1935) and Erik Arup (1876–1951), labelled the expeditions 'Crusades' (*korstog*), the links between the northern Crusades and Crusades elsewhere were not explored. Historians disagreed on the motivation of the Danish kings who promoted the Crusades: whether or not were they driven by a desire to expand Danish territory, to further Danish trade, to convert non-Christians or defend missionaries working in the Baltic lands.

In 1991, Estonia regained its independence after the collapse of the Soviet Union. The 1990s saw much political, economic and cultural collaboration between Denmark and the new republic. Occasionally, the shared past was evoked – or re-imagined – in public speeches and monuments (which did not dwell on the harsh treatment of the Estonians in the High Middle Ages). In the late 1990s, a group of Danish scholars, including Kurt Villads Jensen, inspired by developments in international scholarship on the Crusades and a new emphasis on the diversity of crusading, began re-examining the Danish Crusades. While they focused on the Danish Crusades in the Baltic region, they stressed the correlation between these expeditions and the crusader movement elsewhere, emphasizing their shared Latin Christian Crusade ideology. These scholars successfully brought the Danish Crusades to the attention of both Danish and international historians and have helped foster a new wave of research and scholarly debate.

Literature

Bysted, A. L., K. V. Jensen, C. S. Jensen, and J. H. Lind. *Jerusalem in the North: Denmark and the Baltic Crusades, 1100–1522*. Turnhout, 2012.

Fonnesberg-Schmidt, I. *The Popes and the Baltic Crusades, 1147–1254*. Leiden, 2007.

Møller Jensen, J. *Denmark and the Crusades 1400–1650*. Leiden, 2007.

Murray, A. V. (ed.). *Crusade and Conversion on the Baltic Frontier*. Aldershot, 2001.

Riant, P. *Expéditions et pèlerinages des Scandinaves en Terre sainte au temps des croisades (Expeditions and Pilgrimages of Scandinavians to the Holy Land in the Time of the Crusades)*. Paris, 1865.

3.12 Reconquista as Crusade? – a view from Spain

Luis García-Guijarro Ramos

From the perspective of the Iberian Peninsula in the Middle Ages, the most relevant aspect of the Crusades (*cruzadas*) is their relationship to the *Reconquista*, not to mention the ideological imprints on the conquests in America. Traditional Spanish historiography made the two concepts, *Reconquista* and Crusade, equivalent or tied them closely together, as was the case in José Goñi Gaztambide's seminal book of 1958. This view dominates opinion today. But in all these, and other similar instances, a detailed analysis of the nature of both concepts was absent. Modern studies on the relationship of the Crusades with the Iberian Reconquest, which are highly influenced by Roger Fletcher's article of 1987, have gone one step further. It has been suggested that the principles of the *Reconquista* became an integral part of the Crusade in the second decade of the 12th century. Thus, the great Christian conquests in al-Andalus – from the capture of Zaragoza in 1118 to the final control of the Emirate of Granada by the Catholic Kings in 1492 – were simply Crusades, as Joseph F. O'Callaghan has suggested in several books. This approach also implied that early struggles with Islam in Iberia, the primitive *Reconquista*, had no religious undertones. Only when, in the second half of the 11th century, Gregorian principles reached Iberia and a rigorist Islamic group from North Africa, the Almoravids, controlled al-Andalus did the conflict acquire a distinctive religious character that allowed already well-developed Crusade ideas to structure Christian expansion over Muslim territories in Iberia from that moment onwards.

These set of ideas have been developed into a model that has been uncritically applied to medieval expansionist developments in Iberia and, as a result, distort their nature. However, two main aspects have been overlooked. First, the assumption that Christian struggles with the Muslims had no religious connotations until the 11th century is highly debatable. Second, there has been no effort to distinguish a distinctive Iberian Christian ideology in warfare against Islam from the very inception of the conflict in the 8th century. This set of principles has been devalued by ignoring its religious character at the start, and later by submitting it to the overriding ideas of Crusade. It is obvious that the *Reconquista* had many ideological aspects in common with the latter doctrine; however, it was different from the Crusade and never dissolved into it throughout the Middle Ages. It did in fact structure the ideology of Iberian Christian kings and counts – all of them based territorial expansion on native peninsular principles and only very rarely relied on the Crusades to extend their polities.

Historiographical discussions apart, it is most relevant to set the focus on how the term 'Crusade' has been widely used in everyday language in the second half of the 20th century to the present. In that time span, its meaning has changed from one period to the other, but in all cases it bears little resemblance to the nature of the concept in the Middle Ages. The two basic uses of the word in the modern world, one positive and the other negative, were and have been related to the existence of a well-defined 'enemy' who had to be attacked with concerted action, like Christian warriors did in times past when confronting Muslims. On the other hand, the negative perspective is related to the vanishing of an general 'enemy' and to the development of pacifist outlooks which condemned any violence, specifically violence related to conflicting religious convictions. Franco's ideological use of the term against Republicans in the Spanish Civil War (1936–39) serves as a reminder of the initial positive meaning.

The rivalry with Nazism and later Communism in the 'Cold War' caused the term to be used in a positive way in colloquial speech, as a natural reaction in many Western countries to what was considered evil in the decades after the Second World War. Its use was extended to refer to beneficial global action against far more vague misfortunes like poverty, hunger or cancer. When the Soviet world collapsed and pacifism strengthened as a consequence of the disappearance of a common recognizable enemy, the word Crusade acquired negative undertones, reflecting on the laicism of modern societies, which have great difficulties in understanding not only religious motives, but also concerted actions which might use terms related to what was considered unjustifiable religious violence. Thus, in this context, the term Crusade refers to sheer fundamentalism, which is the opposite image of laicism in the Western world nowadays. This new terminological approach did not change much after 2001, or after the subsequent attacks of radical Islamism against the West (e.g. Madrid 2004). In spite of a certain revival of the word Crusade to define the projected military actions against Islamic terrorism, the use of that concept in this new setting has not taken root; instead, Islamic and Christian fundamentalism are sometimes presented as equivalent.

The positive connotations of the word Crusade in Western societies during a great part of the second half of the 20th century implied meanings which had little to do with the significance of the concept in the Middle Ages. It is even more so in the case of the modern association of the term with fundamentalism.

When addressing the question of the meaning of the Crusades today, it is necessary to distinguish discussions among historians regarding the Crusades in medieval times from the use of the word and variable usage in everyday language in modern Western societies.

Literature

Altamira, R. 'Spain, 1031–1248'. In *The Cambridge Medieval History*, vols. 6, eds. J. R. Tanner, C. W. Previté-Orton, and Z. N. Brooke. Cambridge, 1929, pp. 393–421.

Fletcher, R. A. 'Reconquest and Crusade in Spain, c. 1050–1150', *Transactions of the Royal Historical Society*, 5th ser. 37 (1987) pp. 31–47.

García-Guijarro Ramos, L. 'Christian Expansion in Medieval Iberia: Reconquista or Crusade?' In *The Crusader World*, ed. Adrian Boas. London/New York, 2016, pp. 163–178.

Goñi Gaztambide, J. *Historia de la bula de la cruzada en España (History of the Papal Bull of Crusade in Spain).* Vitoria, 1958.

O'Callaghan, J. F. *The Last Crusade in the West: Castile and the Conquest of Granada*. Philadelphia, 2014.

3.13 The heirs of the first Crusader Kings – a view from Belgium

Thérèse de Hemptinne

What do the medieval Crusades (Croisade/Kruistocht) – i.e. the military expeditions to secure free access to Jerusalem and other Holy loci for Christian pilgrims (11th–15th centuries) – mean in Belgian history, historiography and today's cultural heritage?

The famous historian, Henri Pirenne (1862–1935), did not write a single word concerning the Crusades in his *Histoire de Belgique*. They were only mentioned in his posthumous *Histoire de l'Europe*, yet without any reference to even one of the many illustrious participants linked to the medieval principalities of present-day Belgium. In his view, the Crusades are to be considered total failures, foremost in the case of the Latin Empire of Constantinople.

In the 19th and 20th centuries, however, the newly created kingdom of Belgium, eager to fashion a heroic common past for its citizens, was in search of exemplary historic figures that could embody that past. As in other European countries, patriotic historiography exalted the glory of their own distinguished participants in medieval military expeditions to the Levant. For example, in the early centuries of crusader activity, nearly every count of Flanders, and sometimes even his wife, became a fervent crusader. The legend of the relic of the Holy Blood brought to Bruges by crusader and pilgrim Thierry of Alsace, count of Flanders, is still very popular. The annual procession of the relic on Ascension Day remains a massive touristic attraction. Characters such as Peter the Hermit, Godfrey of Bouillon, the Duke of Lower Lotharingia and Robert Count of Flanders were among the crusaders who took Jerusalem in 1099. Moreover, Baldwin, Count of Flanders/Hainault, was the first Latin emperor of Constantinople in 1204. All of the above-mentioned figures became heroes, and their exploits were taught to children in school. Statues of these 'national' heroes were erected in Huy, Brussels and Mons. Still in the 1950s, a very popular series of chromos trade cards illustrating Belgian History, *Nos Gloires*, pictured them all in their crusaders outfits. Textbooks used in secondary schools in the 21th century still mention them, but with warnings about the ideological, patriotic and colonial bias of previous historiography. They also make sure to take the Arabic point of view into account. Crusades are now presented as one type of the many forms of warfare in medieval times. Certainly, the school population in Brussels, Antwerp, Gent, Liège and other cities of contemporary

Belgium are no longer composed exclusively of Western European, mostly Catholic young people. Therefore, the Crusades are a topic teachers must handle cautiously. The 'Children's Crusade' of 1212 remains popular among Dutch-speaking adolescents, due to a successful young adult novel by Thea Beckman, *Kruistocht in spijkerbroek* ('Crusade in jeans'). This novel has been translated into many European languages and even had a movie by Ben Sombogaart as well as a musical based on it.

In the second half of the 20th century, the historiography of the Crusades did not rank high on the list of priorities for scholarly historical research in Belgium. The regionalization of the country in an ongoing process of state reforms resulted in a paradigmatic shift in the country's historiography. A national point of view gave way to a much greater emphasis on regional history (of Flanders, of Wallonia or of the Low Countries, which implies both Belgium and the Netherlands). Interest in the regional actors of the Crusades and military orders based in these territories decreased, the period from the 11th up to the 13th century was dealt with the most, except for the so-called 'Burgundian' period. After the fall of Constantinople in 1453, the ideal of the Crusades flared up briefly. The history of the Crusades and crusaders was dealt with by academic historians sporadically, mainly in the context of research on other topics in medieval history, or indirectly in the context of source editions or of art exhibitions. In general, scholars from abroad, such as Jean Flori, Alan V. Murray, Nicholas Paul and Jonathan Phillips, carry the torch of studies on the Crusades, even giving attention to the contribution of our 'national' actors. Only the Latin Empire and its 'Belgian' emperors seem to have continued to inspire our academic historians.

Belgian archives, libraries and museums are repositories for many different sources on the Crusades (see *Narrative sources* and *Diplomata belgica*). A unique treasure of 13th-century goldsmith's art that was made by Hugo of Oignies and his workshop, which was destined to hold precious relics imported from the Levant by crusaders and pilgrims, is on display in the *Musée provincial* in Namur. Many similar artefacts are kept in Belgian churches, chapels and museums. They are palpable testimonies of the importance of our crusader heritage. However, these are not always well known by the general public.

There are, in fact, no descendants of known crusaders who play any role in Belgian politics or social life. However, members of the royal family still bear titles of the medieval territorial princes (Brabant, Flanders, Hainaut, etc.), and many noble families are members of the Order of Malta.

Literature

Diplomata Belgica. URL: www.diplomata-belgica.be; Narrative Sources. URL: www.narrative-sources.be.

Hendrickx, B. On the 'Belgian' Emperors of Constantinople: A Book in Greek, Thessaloniki, 1970, and Several Articles in the Seventies and Eighties, Among Them: 'Régestes des empereurs latins de Constantinople (1204–1261/1272)' (Regestas of the Latin Emperors of Constantinople), *Byzantina* 14 (1988), pp. 7–221.

Morelli, A. (ed.) *Les grands mythes de l'histoire de Belgique, de Flandre et de Wallonie (The great Myths of the History of Belgium, Flanders and Wallonia)*. Brussels, 1995.

Smet, J.-J. de. *Mémoire sur Robert de Jérusalem, comte de Flandre à la première croisade (Memoir on Robert of Jerusalem, count of Flanders at the First Crusade)*, (Mémoires de l'Académie royale, t. XXXII) Brussels, 1861.

Tricht, F. Van. *The Latin Renovatio of Byzantium: the Empire of Constantinople (1204–1228)*. Leiden, 2011.

Verlinden, C. *Les empereurs belges de Constantinople (The Belgian Emperors of Constantinople)*. Brussels, 1945.

3.14 In the light and shadow of Richard the Lionheart – a view from the United Kingdom

Mike Horswell and Jonathan Phillips

The memory and legacy of the Crusades in the United Kingdom is a complex and, at times, contradictory story. Comfortably, the most famous crusader in British history is Richard the Lionheart, immortalized in the statue standing outside the House of Commons since 1860. He is, by popular repute, a brave and mighty warrior, although also seen as an absentee king and therefore a poor ruler. No other crusaders, British or otherwise, have a comparable presence in contemporary memory culture in Great Britain.

The subject of the Crusades has had a chequered history, with the Enlightenment period casting the movement in a highly negative light; Hume (1761), 'the most durable monument to human folly that has yet appeared in any age or nation', or Gibbon (1788), saw them as 'caused by a savage fanaticism' that 'checked rather than forwarded the maturity of Europe'. In the 19th century, however, two additional factors came into play. First, the cultural movement known as the Gothic revival meant a new enthusiasm for the medieval period; secondly, western political powers returned to the Near East. As a result of these points, the idea of the Crusades re-emerged strongly in a number of arenas. It was seen as sufficiently flexible to incorporate contemporary cultural themes, such as the Romantic reaction to industrialization, the rise of popular imperialism and the cult of chivalry. The enormously successful novels of Sir Walter Scott (notably *The Talisman*, 1825) and subsequent pictures, plays, music, opera and novels engaged with the Crusades, where they were often replayed as a chivalric, romantic venture.

In parallel with religious uses (i.e. in contexts of missionary work), we can find fully secular uses of the word meaning a good cause, or a purpose with a moral right. Self-evidently, some of these can be political in context: a 'Crusade' for Brexit or a 'Crusade' for more grammar schools.

While the formal apparatus of a papal appeal to authorize a Crusade no longer operated, numerous military endeavours employed the imagery of a crusader and harnessed the idea of a noble struggle, possibly with God's blessing, and certainly of positive moral value. The First World War is the clearest example of this: Prime Minister Lloyd George spoke of the war as a 'great Crusade' in a speech to his constituents in May 1916. When General Allenby entered Jerusalem in

1917, the press enthusiastically embraced the parallels to the medieval Crusades and to the presence of Richard the Lionheart in the Holy Land. Allenby's campaign was popularly remembered as 'The Last Crusade', while war memorials often made use of a 'crusader's' sword on the cross of sacrifice. Interwar organizations drew on crusading rhetoric and imagery to frame their purposes: there were fascist, socialist, pacifist and Catholic 'Crusades' in the 1920s and 1930s. Similarly, the Most Noble Order of Crusaders was formed in 1921 as an organization for ex-servicemen of all social backgrounds, although it faded into obscurity before the Second World War.

There is some mention of the idea in the discourse surrounding the Second World War, but far less than before. Early attempts by the British government to employ the Crusades for propaganda purposes were abortive and seemed to lack traction with the public. The Eighth Army's Operation Crusader in 1941 in North Africa and various army units' patches which featured crusader swords kept the military connection in play, however superficially.

It seems that the notion had slipped into a broad cultural consciousness meaning a good cause, or else casting back to something far back in history. It could, therefore, comfortably fit into television shows or computer games and has been an immensely popular subject for novels throughout the 20th century to the present. The memory of the crusading era is referenced in the Premiership Rugby team, Saracens, founded in 1876 'named after the famous desert warriors led by Saladin', and the Northern Irish football team 'Crusaders' (est. 1896).

Academic interest in the subject emerged strongly in the aftermath of Sir Steven Runciman's vivid but critical *A History of the Crusades*. Large numbers of scholars, many under the direction of Jonathan Riley-Smith (d.2016), emerged to research and publish on the subject. This, coupled with evermore texts in translation, has meant a greater interest in the subject and accessibility of materials to teach the Crusades at schools and universities. The major 'A' level examination boards and other qualifications all feature modules on the Crusades and are taken across a relatively small but significant number of schools and sixth-form colleges. Likewise, many university History Departments offer courses covering aspects of the Crusades.

In this century, the emergence of conflicts with Al-Qaeda and ISIS has done much to heighten interest in the subject and to raise awareness of the potentially charged nature of invoking imagery that, in a British context, has come to mean a positive cause, or else refers to events from many centuries back. Yet to many in the Near East, it is a synonym for Western aggression and conquest.[13] The legacy of conflict with Islam is also, of course, ripe to be used by Far-Right extremists and examples of this can be found on the internet with ease. With Britain now a multi-cultural society, these different receptions of the history and meaning of the Crusades need to be understood, as they form part of the patchwork of the memory of the Crusades in 21st-century Britain.

Literature

Horswell, M. J. *The Rise and Fall of British Crusader Medievalism, c.1825 to 1945*. Abingdon, 2018.

Phillips, J. P. *Holy Warriors: A Modern History of the Crusades*. London, 2009.

Riley-Smith, J. *What Were the Crusades?* Houndmills/Basingstoke/New York, 1977.

Runciman, S. *A History of the Crusades*. Cambridge, 1950–1954.

Siberry, E. *The New Crusaders: Images of the Crusades in the 19th and Early 20th Centuries*. Aldershot, 2000.

Tyerman, C. J. *The Debate on the Crusades*. Manchester, 2011.

Selected popular item:

Scott, W. *The Talisman*. Edinburgh, 1825.

3.15 A state of continuous rape and violation – a view from Syria

Mohamad Isa

"Wake up Saladin, we are back again!" proclaimed the French general Henri Gouraud as he kicked the grave of Saladin in Damascus in 1920. In this way, according to the master narrative prescribed by the Ba'ath Party in Syria, the French general mocked the Sultan who decisively defeated the crusaders in 1187 at the Battle of Hattin. From this perspective, the French occupation of Syria after the First World War appears to be part of an unbroken continuation of the Crusades. They did not end with the expulsion of the last Latins from Acre in 1291. Instead, the Crusades lived on in multiple forms, such as colonialism or the Balfour Declaration (1926), as well as the Israeli-Zionists occupation of Palestine that followed.

There is no explicit position on the Crusades held by the Ba'ath Party. However, the basic policy programme of the party regards the Near East as an Arab region and endorses the Arabic people defending their land and property against Zionism and Western colonialism. The overriding principle is that the Arabic people are a single nation and have the natural right to live in a unified, common state. The third principle of the party's programme is that the Arabic nation considers all colonial intentions as criminal. Furthermore, such intentions are to be fought against in order to defend or liberate the Arabic homeland. A clear view of the perspective is present in the foundational works of Syrian historiographers who follow the party's ideology. An example of this would be Soheil Zakkar, the author of a four-volume encyclopaedia of the Crusades, which is an important reference work on the Crusades. According to Zakkar, his motivations to write the book were purely academic. Nevertheless, they were profoundly influenced by the Zionistic population of the Levant as well as by the Crusades against the Arabic Nation and the other Muslim peoples. In addition, he expresses his gratitude to the support for the research and printing of the encyclopaedia to the former Syrian president, Hafez al-Assad, who at that time was the secretary general of the Syrian Ba'ath Party. In his book, he praises the Arabs of the time of the Middle Ages as freedom fighters and heroes, as well as their worthy successor and paternal defender of all Arabic people, the President Hafez al-Assad.

What was the reason that the call to Crusade by Pope Urban II resonated with the Europeans, so much so that hundreds of thousands of them marched to the East? From whence did the terrible hate come that led the participants of the First Crusades to not only desire to exterminate the Arabs, but even to eat their flesh (Maalouf)?

These questions that the entirety of the Syrian society asks regarding the Crusades are because of the influence of the Ba'ath Party, which is viewed as the leader of the state as well as society. In this sense, colonialism and Zionism are continuations of the Crusades. It is astounding how in so many cases the mindset of the Arabs – and Muslims in general today – is influenced by events from centuries ago. On the other hand, since the third millennium, political and religious leaders in the Arab world have continued to demand the reconquest of Jerusalem and the destruction of the State of Israel, which is referred to as a crusader state in official speeches.

In the Islamic world, which is attacked repeatedly since the past, there is an inescapable feeling of persistent, growing oppression. Every form of danger is quite often interpreted by oppressed people as the confirmation of constant colonial ambitions of the West in the Arab world. They also see every military conflict through the lens of East and West; thus, the Arabs have the feeling of being in a state of continuous rape and violation.

Like all the powers that support dictators in the Arab world, the Ba'ath Party utilizes propaganda against the people they rule. For instance, they justify existing abuses – such as a shortage economy, poverty, unemployment, all general social injustices, as well as the prevention of democratic constitutions, political repression and economic exploitation – by arguing that Western colonialism is to blame.

Literature

Maalouf, A. *The Crusades through Arab Eyes*. London, 2012.

Spuler, Bertold, Khaled Asaad Issa, Soheil Zakkar. *Al aalam al islami fi al asr al maghuli (History of the Islam World: The Time of the Mongols)*. Damascus, 1982.

3.16 The deplorable Crusades – a view from Sweden

Kurt Villads Jensen

In Sweden, historians have normally investigated three different crusading movements in the Middle Ages: those to the Middle East, the Baltic Crusades and the Swedish Crusades to Finland.

The Crusades to the Middle East began with the conquest of Jerusalem in 1099, which led to the establishment of the Latin Kingdom of Jerusalem and a number of crusader principalities. Swedish research and general textbooks are only rarely concerned with the later medieval attempts to launch Crusades to Jerusalem or against the Ottoman Empire. Few sources attest to Swedish participation in the Middle Eastern Crusades.

Scandinavian historiography during the 20th century has concentrated on political, economic and material explanations. The Crusades have been depicted as papal attempts to gain secular power, as Latin Europeans being attracted by the riches of the Middle East, or as the only means of making an independent living for the sons of the aristocracy. Several historians have understood the Crusades as an early example of European colonialism.

The Crusades to the Baltic were, in a Swedish context, primarily directed against Lithuania, Livonia and Estonia,[14] while the Danish historical tradition has also been interested in Crusades to Northern Germany. Because of the sources, the best studied period is from around 1200 until the mid-14th century, but the Crusades continued in some form until the Lutheran Reformation in the first half of the 16th century. After the Reformation, both Swedish and Danish kings presented themselves as defenders of the true faith, e.g. during the Thirty Years War. They continued to utilize the rhetoric of religious warfare similar to that of the medieval Crusades.

The main actors in the Baltic Crusades were the Danes[15] and the Teutonic Order.[16] However, Swedes also participated. In the 14th century, Sweden conducted a spectacular but unsuccessful Crusade against Novgorod. King Magnus Eriksson (1316–74) marched under a banner depicting Christ and a sword, essentially offering the Novgorodians the choice between converting to Latin Catholicism or war, but he lost those battles. These Crusades have been explained by power politics and attempts to gain control over the Russian trading routes through the Baltics and Russia. The religious justification has normally been considered only superficial or a pretext.

The Crusades to Finland have been important in Finnish historiography as elements leading to the Europeanization of Finland.[17] In Swedish historiography, their significance has been significantly downplayed. The creation of the common Swedish–Finnish realm (which existed until 1809) has been explained as a long-term Swedish colonization of Finland that began before the period of the Crusades. Swedish and Finnish historians debate whether the so-called First Crusade to Finland in around 1155 ever took place, or if it is a hagiographic fabrication of the late 13th century that was created to support the cult of the king, Saint Eric of Sweden. Two larger expeditions, one from 1238 to 1240 and the other from 1292 to 1323, are better substantiated. They are traditionally labelled the Second and Third Crusade to Finland, but were in reality part of regular expeditions.

Medieval Crusades against heretics are dismissed in Sweden as solely political; and apparently there were no heretics in Sweden in the Middle Ages.

Modern historiography operates with the view that there are no Crusades in present-day Sweden, and any significant influence of crusading ideology has only been recently pointed out. The Hospitallers were the only military crusading order in Scandinavia (with the exception of the Teutonic Order having one small house in Sweden), but their integration into, and significance for, Swedish society has only been studied superficially. Saint Bridget of Sweden (died in 1373) received revelations that included exhortations to, and justification for, crusading that she passed on to the Swedish king. This aspect of her revelations has also been given relatively little scholarly attention.

In present-day Swedish society, the Crusades are generally seen as a deplorable misunderstanding of Christianity, and the term 'Crusade' (*korståg*, 'cross expedition') has not been used as a designation for any broad movement to support good causes as it has in many other countries. To a greater extent than before, since the late 1990s, some historians have begun to discuss the religious elements in medieval crusading and treat Swedish and Baltic Crusades parallel to the Middle Eastern Crusades. This development was part of a general internationalization of Scandinavian historical research.

Crusades have been important in popular culture, e.g. in novels such as Jan Guillou's on the Templar *Arn*, 1998–2001, and movies, like Bergman's *The Seventh Seal* from 1957, or Arn in 2008, which had the largest budget ever for a film in the Nordic countries at that time. Since around 1990, there has been an explosion in medievalism, with centres and re-enactments. For example, the annual medieval week on

Gotland has around 40,000 participants and includes many themes featuring the Crusades.

Historians in Sweden have not begun to explain the medieval Crusades as the necessary defence against the inherently violent religion of Islam, as has happened internationally in some cases since 2001.

Literature

Carlsson, C. On Archaeology of Crusades and Military Orders, also in Sweden, Several Articles and the Ph.D. dissertation: *Johanniterordens kloster i Skandinavien 1291–1536. En studie av deras ekonomiska förhållanden utifrån historiskt och arkeologiskt material (The Convents of the order of St John in Scandinavia 1291–1536. A historical and archaeological study of their economy)*. Odense, 2009. www.google.se/search?client=safari&rls=en&q=carlsson+Johanniterordens+kloster+i+Skandinavien+1291-1536,+Odense+2009&ie=UTF-8&oe=UTF-8&gfe_rd=cr&ei=wy9AV_rXH6Or8wfmmYvICQ.

Harrison, D. Contributions to Several Textbooks, and Author of a Monograph on Nordic Crusades: *Gud vill det! Nordiska korsfarare under medeltiden (God Wills It! Nordic Crusaders in the Middle Ages)*. Lund, 2006.

Lindkvist, T. Contributions to Several Textbooks, and Several Articles, e.g. 'Legitimisation of Power and Crusades as Europeanisation in Medieval Sweden'. In *The Reception of Medieval Europe in the Baltic Sea Region*, ed. Jörn Staecker, Papers of the XIIth Visby Symposium held at Gotland University, (Acta Visbyensia, 12). Visby, 2009, pp. 33–41.

3.17 Neither Rome nor Baghdad: the Crusades – a view from Ireland

Conor Kostick

Irish crusading historiography is heavily influenced by I.S. Robinson, former Lecky Chair of History at Trinity College Dublin. It is largely the case that Irish scholars who publish and present research on the Crusades – such as Léan Ní Chléirigh, Conor McCann, Axel Kelly and myself – are former PhD researchers of Professor Robinson. Two other notable centres for Crusade-related research in Ireland are UCD, where Edward Coleman's work on Italian cities has a Crusade-connection and Galway, where Kimberly LoPrete's interests include the Crusades. But overall, there are relatively few Irish scholars researching the subject, and this perhaps reflects the low level of participation by people from Ireland in the medieval Crusades.

In his research and mentoring (although less evident in his publications), I.S. Robinson gives great attention to the ideological development of the crusading idea and, in particular, how the reform papacy began to espouse the notion of the legitimacy of knights fighting for God. In this regard, he sees the Carl Erdmann thesis as significant. In 1935, Erdmann argued that when the 11th-century reform papacy changed the notion of a *miles Christi* from a Christian who metaphorically fought for God to the one who actually took up arms, the most important step towards crusading was taken.

I.S. Robinson also developed the views of H.E.J. Cowdrey: that the Peace of God and Truce of God play an important part in the process of gestation that leads to the Crusades. This emphasis on evolutions in medieval thought dovetails with the approach of Jonathan Riley-Smith in his later writings, and it is no coincidence that Robinson, Riley-Smith and Cowdrey were collaborators for the *New Cambridge Medieval History VI, c.1024 – c.1198.*

Another similarity of method between these historians is that of close prosopographical investigation. In Robinson's case, his research does not simply concern a close reading of medieval texts in order to detect innovation but also a consideration of the networks of medieval people who took up and championed new ideas. This means that Irish scholars have been encouraged to fuse continental traditions of structural analysis into discussion of key crusading sources, albeit in a rather more detailed, case-study basis than can be found in the writings of figures such as Bloch and Duby.

If one can generalize from so few examples, Irish scholars tend to read crusading sources with a high sensitivity to the context of a reform papacy struggling to reorganize the church (e.g. Léan Ní Chléirigh's reading of Fulcher of Chartres in 'The impact of the First Crusade' or my own assessment of the early Crusade sources in *The Social Structure of the First Crusade*). An emphasis on the importance of the ideological struggles within Christendom makes for a certain amount of scepticism over the motives of the crusaders and – again with the caveat that there are only a few examples – Ireland probably lies closer to continental Europe than to the Anglo-American schools of thought, which were dominant in the early years of the new millennium. I would say this is quite distinct in my own work.

In respect to the question of Islam and the Muslim world, the major influence in Ireland is probably not academic. Having escaped an empire in its own past, Ireland's citizens, broadly speaking, are mistrustful of the motives of superpowers. Thus, although Ireland historically has been a very Catholic nation, there is no automatic inclination by those teaching the subject to identify with the crusaders and against Muslims. If anything, an appreciation exists here that in the age of the Crusades, the greatest libraries, the most dramatic advances in science and culture and the most vivid literature was to be found outside of Christendom.

There is little attention paid to the Crusades in Irish schoolbooks or in cultural productions, such as films or historical novels. And this is almost certainly a legacy of a highly politicized divide over medieval studies, with early 20th-century republicans seeing the arrival of the Normans and their world (which would be closely associated with the Crusades) as a disaster for Ireland's subsequent fate. For example, one of the leaders of the Easter Rising of 1916, Michael O'Hanrahan (Miceál Ua hAnnracáin), wrote a historical novel, *When the Norman Came*, in order to create in literature youthful examples of heroic Irish warriors who fought bravely and with honour against the invader.

Literature

Kostick, C. *The Siege of Jerusalem: Conquest and Crusade in 1099*. London, 2009.

Kostick, C. *The Social Structure of the First Crusade*. Leiden, 2008.

Ní Chléirigh, L. 'Anti-Byzantine polemic in the Dei Gesta per Francos of Guibert, Abbot of Nogent-sous-Coucy'. In *Sailing to Byzantium*, ed. Savvas Neocleous. Newcastle, 2009, pp. 53–76.

Ní Chléirigh, L. 'The Impact of the First Crusade on Western Opinion Towards the Byzantine Empire: the Dei Gesta per Francos of Guibert of Nogent and the Historia Hierosolymitana of Fulcher of Chartres'. In *The Cruades and the Near East: Cultural Histories*, ed. Conor Kostick, London, 2011, pp. 161–188.

Robinson, I. S. 'Reform and the Church, 1073–1122'. In *New Cambridge Medieval History IV: c.1024–c.1198*, eds. D. Luscombe and J. Riley-Smith. Cambridge, 1999, pp. 268–394.

Ua hAnnracáin, M. *When the Norman Came.* Dublin, 2015 [1918].

3.18 For too long French historians were not critical enough – a (second) view from France[18]

Guy Lobrichon

[The editors would like to thank Dr. Miriam Sénécheau for her valuable help with the translation.]

'Crusade', what a unique and not entirely innocuous concept that is politically incorrect today! The French expression for 'Crusade' arose in the 14th century, more than two centuries after the beginning of the historical phenomenon that it describes, i.e. the military conquest of the tomb of Christ, Jerusalem and holy sites (1098–1099). It is true that the Crusades have a precursor in the Occident, but the term *crozata* appears around 1215 as the designation for the royal army in the Albigensian Crusade. Over time, the concept of 'Crusade' has taken on a different meaning. It came to mean a holy war waged for control of the Holy Land, involving fighting against the 'unbelieving' occupiers of the Near East, Egypt and the Ottoman Empire. It then took on the meaning of a religious war to impose by force one dominant religious model over another ("Catharism", 16th century Reforms); it was used to justify territorial conquests and, in the south of France since the 19th century, to legitimize resistance to the centralizing state; French vocabulary applies it today by extension to anti-Western ideologies of religious origin, Islamism or Hinduism. The example of the Latin Kingdom of Jerusalem (1101–1291) shows, from the first decades, the malleability of Western models. Early on, this idea was supercharged with religiosity; yet, its religiosity cannot cover up the reality of violence, not then and not today.

The historian cannot remain silent in the face of the contemporary reclaiming and retelling that attempt to connect the far off past of the 11th and 12th centuries – which were characterized by uncontrollable actions of the world powers – with the present. Those who attempt to make this connection dream of restoring order in accordance with old and past ideas. Was this not the intention of those in the 11th and 12th centuries who created the concept that they called, 'Christendom'?

It is no longer possible to speak and to write about the Crusades without denouncing, indicting or clarifying a remarkable past, which Western societies too easily accept. This was not the problem of the French historians when they rekindled knowledge of the Crusades during Napoleon's expedition to Egypt. They revived a topic that had been hidden ever since the Battle of Lepanto. In the very moment that the French took possession of Algeria (1830–1848), these historians resolved to take up the publication of the *Recueil des Historiens des Croisades*, which still influences contemporary academic research. This resulted in the concept being limited to the expeditions to the Holy Land for far too long.

One of the consequences of this was that the concept of Crusade – typical for the 19th century – remained closely connected to the notion of 'Christendom', sharing a connection to the enterprise of colonialism. Both were conceived as advancing civilization. The activity of the future Cardinal Lavigerie in Algeria from 1868 and the intervention of the "Papal Zouaves" in the defence of the Papal States in 1869–1870 bear witness to this in two different ways. Moreover, structuralism – which dominated during 1960 to 1970 – had strongly affected the circles of French historians (or more simply: French historians). Here, the subject of 'Crusades' was largely marginalized, as it was equated with the history of slaughter (e.g. the founder of the *Annales* discredited them). However, conscious of this danger, some have directed their attention to the trans-Mediterranean (Jean Richard, Michel Balard), while others have allowed themselves to be led by an inglorious neo-positivism (René Grousset).

Essentially, this means that our tools and our way of thinking warrant critical self-reflection, of which we are still waiting. The expansion of the concept of Crusades into regions boarding Spain and the Baltic states was not the result of the work of French historians. There is an overt silence by the French historians regarding the contamination of the idea of Crusades with political ideas from the Middle Ages and the present. The investigation of the First Crusade is symptomatic of this situation. When some of the chroniclers of that time (e.g. Sigebert of Gembloux) denounced the expedition from 1096 to 1099 as a popular movement, they were covering up the Crusades involvement in the Investiture Controversy. The Pope's interference is disqualified due to the Doctrine of Pope Gelasius, which stipulated the separation of the two authorities – the spiritual authority and secular authority. Paul Alphandéry and Alphonse Dupront, as well as Jean Flori all took up this problematic. The work on the far-reaching repercussions of the as of yet too little critically reflected upon concept must be carried forward, following the example of Anglo-American historians.

Literature

Alphandéry, P. et Alphonse Dupront. *La chrétienté et l'idée de croisade (The Christendom and the Idea of Crusading)*, 2 vols. Paris, Albin Michel, 1954–1959.

Buc, P. *Holy War, Martyrdom, and Terror. Christianity, Violence, and the West*. Philadelphia, 2015.

Cassidy-Welch, M. and A. E. Lester, 'Memory and Interpretation: New Approaches to the Study of the Crusades', *Journal of Medieval History* 40:3 (2014), pp. 225–236.

Flori, J. *Croisade et chevalerie, XIe-XIIe siècles (Crusade and Knighthood, 11th-12th Centuries)*. Bruxelles, 1998.

3.19 In the frontiers of the former kingdom of Jerusalem: risk of misunderstandings – a view from Israel

Sophia Menache

Yvonne Friedman, in discussing the main characteristics of Israeli crusader historiography, calls attention to the inner dialogue between research of the Crusades and contemporary reality. This link further substantiates, in her view, a differentiation between Israelis and other researchers in the field. Such differentiation can, indeed, easily be justified from a geophysical perspective. Crusader castles, fortresses, churches and manor houses are an integral component of the Israeli landscape and, as such, are part and parcel of the daily experience of Israeli historians. It is not the human factor but the geographical – since Jews did not participate in the Crusades but were their victims – that creates the primary differentiation between the Israeli historians' perspective of the Crusades and those of others.

The association between the Crusades and the State of Israel, however, also has risks. Comparison with the Crusades – with an emphasis on their provisional nature – has characterized Islamic radical and fundamentalist propaganda for the past one hundred years. With or without their contemporaneous nuances, the Crusades and the Christian settlements in the Latin East represent one of the main streams of Israeli historical research, which is closely related to the late Joshua Prawer (1917–1990). Indeed, his main achievement was to turn the Crusades into an independent domain of research, while focusing on the classical period – from Urban II's call in Clermont in 1095 until the fall of crusader Acre in 1291. Following Prawer's approach, much of Israeli crusader historiography focuses on the two-hundred-year existence of the crusader Kingdom of Jerusalem. Similarly, most Israeli historians followed Prawer's approach and restricted the definition of Crusade to those expeditions whose ultimate goal was to conquer or secure the Holy Land.

Research on crusader society led Prawer to posit the existence of an 'apartheid' (e.g. a colonial) society, whose lack of knowledge of, or interest in its neighbours eventually brought about its collapse. However, strong emphasis on the interplay of archaeological evidence and documentary testimonies led to the rejection of Prawer's segregation model, while revealing cross-cultural influences between the conquerors and the conquered. The well-known passage of Fulcher of Chartres, "*For we who were Occidentals have now become Orientals. He who was a Roman or a Frank has in this land been made into a Galilean, or a Palestinian […]*" (*Historia Iherosolymitana*, l. III, 37: 2–8), hints at this interaction and faithfully reflects the history of the State of Israel as it is characterized by a continuous process of immigration from different countries all over the world.

Since the Crusades actually represent the meeting point among opposing religions/cultures/societies, crusader research investigates the perception of the 'other' as well. This is a crucial subject for understanding Israeli society in general and the conflict with the Palestinians in particular.

The Crusades have been perceived as foreshadowing the traumatic persecution of Jews in Europe – which began in 1096, parallel to, if not a result of the First Crusade – and the tormented Jewish history of the 20th century. Furthermore, the analogy between the Crusades and the Zionist movement has become an integral part of Israeli intellectual discourse. While anti-Zionists use the Crusade analogy to depict the State of Israel as a colonial project, many Israelis deny such a link, emphasizing the inherent differences between the Zionist movement and the Crusades. The Crusades are nonetheless present in a variety of ways within Israeli intellectual discourse: they serve as a source of inspiration for novels, poetry and literature at large. For example, A. B. Yehoshua, *In Front of the Forest* (1963), Itzhak Shalev, *The Case of Gabriel Tirosh* (1964) and Amos Oz, *Unto Death* (1971).

Still, Israeli research on the Crusades reflects a gap, and even a detachment, between ideological or political discourse, on the one hand, and historical research, on the other. This separation should perhaps be regarded as a reproduction of the well-known convergence/divergence phenomenon between collective memory and historical research. The discourse surrounding the Crusades played a role in constructing Israeli collective memory. At the same time, however, the historiography of the Crusades was an important element in the scholarly attempt to overcome the shadows of the collective memory and guarantee the autonomy of scientific research. Intellectual discourse was less interested in the history of the Crusades as they were in their ideological and moral ramifications. The politicization of the Crusades thus turned them into a sort of 'usable past' that, like other forms of usable past exploited by national movements, was adapted to serve ideological and political needs. Israeli intellectual discourse, as a result, has isolated the Crusades from their medieval framework and analysed them in the context of the modern Israeli-Arab conflict. Israeli historians, in contrast, analyse the Crusades as an integral part of medieval history, thus underlining the struggle between collective memory and historical research. Therefore, research of the crusader period was not a continuation of the political debate, but its very opposite. Employing scrupulous research, Israeli scholars liberated crusader images, terms and history from their modern ideological and political categories. In order to counterbalance the influence of the crusader heritage in the Israeli collective memory, there was a need for meticulous historical research that would suggest not only an additional but also an authoritative narrative.

Literature

Ellenblum, R. *Frankish Rural Settlement in the Latin Kingdom of Jerusalem.* Cambridge, 1998.

Friedman, Y. *Encounter between Enemies: Captivity and Ransom in the Latin Kingdom of Jerusalem.* Leiden, 2002.

Kedar, B. *Crusade and Mission: European Approaches toward the Muslims.* Princeton, 1984.

Kedar, B. *Franks, Muslims and Oriental Christians in the Latin Levant: Studies in Frontier Acculturation.* Aldershot, 2006.

Prawer, J. *A History of the Latin Kingdom of Jerusalem*, 2 vols. Jerusalem, 1963–1971.

Prawer, J. *The Latin Kingdom of Jerusalem: European Colonialism in the Middle Ages.* London, 1972.

Prawer, J. *Crusader Institutions.* Oxford, 1980.

3.20 Fighting at the Nile between history and fantasy – a view from the Netherlands

Jaap van Moolenbroek

When in 1095 Pope Urban II urged western Christians to liberate the Holy Sepulchre in Jerusalem, his call for an armed pilgrimage found little resonance in the area of the present-day Netherlands. This changed when Jerusalem, captured during the First Crusade in 1099, was recaptured by Muslim ruler Saladin in 1187. The subsequent Third Crusade (1189–1192) saw a significant number of participants from this area for the first time. The vast majority consisted of Frisians: inhabitants of the northern coastal areas along the North Sea, for the most part living in present-day Dutch territory. The Frisians continued to take part in the Crusades all the way through the last general expedition of 1270. Each time, they made the whole journey by sea, usually with about fifty ships ('cogs'). Their main contribution to the war effort was during the Fifth Crusade (1217–1221), at the siege of the Egyptian city of Damietta.[19] At the time, the town was protected by a tower in the Nile and a chain spanning from this tower to one of the city's wall towers. Following a design of Oliver of Paderborn, scholaster of Cologne Cathedral – who had preached the Crusade in the Rhineland and Frisia, as well as participated in the expedition himself – the Frisians transformed two of their cogs into a siege craft with a huge scaling ladder. Then, in August 1218, they used this structure to take the Nile tower, accompanied by fighters from other countries. No mention is made of Count William I of Holland whose reign covered the western region of the present-day Netherlands and who also participated in the expedition, taking an active role. After the fall of the chain tower, most Frisians returned home, as did Count William of Holland the following summer. In November 1219, the city itself was conquered, only to be lost again in 1221.

Two centuries of silence later, Damietta unexpectedly became a familiar sound in current Dutch territory, as a result of two stories which entered into circulation at that time. First, around 1450, the contribution of the Frisians to the capture of the Nile tower was embellished as part of a series of legendary stories that drew a parallel between the history of the Frisians and that of the people of Israel in the Old Testament. As God had performed great deeds through Israel, he had also done through the Frisians, and Damietta in 1218 was no exception.

Second, and much more influential, was a myth created around 1400 in Haarlem, the second city of the county of Holland. Here, the conquest of Damietta was linked to the Third Crusade and the Emperor Frederick I Barbarossa. According to this story, the emperor could only conquer the chain-protected harbour of Damietta, thanks to an action by crusaders from Haarlem, along with young William of Holland, the future Count. They attached toothed iron to the bow and keel of a sailing ship and sailed the harbour chain into pieces, allowing the city to be captured. As a reward, the Haarlem crusaders received a new coat of arms for their city from the hands of the emperor and the patriarch of Jerusalem. This story, having no basis in historical reality, became accepted as history in the county of Holland within a century, gradually spreading throughout the other regions of the Netherlands. When, after 1600, it became clear that Damietta had not been conquered around 1190, but in 1219, the myth was gradually and reluctantly abandoned. Nevertheless, the false belief that Damietta had been captured by the 'Dutch' under Count William I of Holland persisted until the late 19th century. It was even taught in schools at the time.

Generally, the Crusades (Dutch: '*kruistochten*') to the East continued to be valued until the early 20th century, with Christian and national views serving as major contributors. After about 1960, the moral validity of the Crusades became increasingly controversial in the public opinion. The age-old alliance of cross and sword was rejected by modern Christians. Pugnacious stories for young people about the Crusade to Damietta made way for a highly successful book by Thea Beckman, first published in 1973, about a boy from Holland who ends up in the Children's Crusade of 1212 – an expedition without any combat between Christians and Muslims. By now, in Dutch public sentiment, the Crusades to Jerusalem seem to have lost all validity. The conviction that Western crusaders went to the East with the primary purpose to fight 'Islam', rather than to retake the Holy Land from non-Christians is widespread. In newspapers and magazines, the former crusader states of the 12th century have been compared more than once with the 'IS' (Islamic State) of our time. On June 20th, 2015, the Dutch quality newspaper *Trouw* ran a full-page historical article with the headline (translated from Dutch), "When Christians founded their 'CS'", containing the subtitle 'The crusaders' thirst of blood yielded in nothing to that of the present-day IS warriors'. Medievalists try to retain a balanced perspective on the Crusades, taking into account their historical context. As a result, there is a considerable divide between popular and scholarly views of the Crusades.

Literature

Mol, J. A. 'Frisian Fighters and the Crusade', *Crusades*, 1 (2002), pp. 89–110.

Moolenbroek, J. van. *Nederlandse kruisvaarders naar Damiate aan de Nijl. Acht eeuwen geschiedenis en fantasie in woord en beeld (Dutch Crusaders to Damietta on the Nile. Eight centuries of History and Fantasy in Text and Image)*. Hilversum, 2016.

Selected popular item:

Beckman, T. *Kruistocht in spijkerbroek (Crusade in Jeans)*. Rotterdam, 1973, 94th impression 2019. Translated in about fifteen languages. The first part of the book was adapted into the Dutch movie *Kruistocht in spijkerbroek (Crusade in Jeans)*, directed by Ben Sombogaart, 2006. Since 2000, a Dutch musical has also been shown in Dutch that is based on the book, with a script by Marc Veerkamp, music by Jeroen Sleyfer.

3.21 The destiny of the West. America and the Crusades – a view from the USA

Mark Gregory Pegg

Today, it is unavoidable that the series of medieval holy wars, now known as the 'Crusades', are seen through the perspective of the aftermath of the terrorist attacks on New York in 2001 and the American-led invasion of Iraq in 2003. Five days after the destruction of the World Trade Center in New York, then President George W. Bush observed, "this Crusade, this war on terrorism is going to take a while".[20] During the recent 2016 American presidential campaign, then candidate Donald J. Trump, while avoiding the word 'Crusade', explicitly framed the terrorism associated with violent extremists in the Middle East and Europe within the 'clash of civilizations' narrative established – mostly by American conservative politicians and scholars, but not completely – since the beginning of this century. It is a cruel irony that Al-Qaeda (and its offshoots), the Taliban in Afghanistan and Isis in Syria and Iraq also frame their attacks on soldiers and civilians of Western democracies as a continuation of the holy war against the Latin Christian crusaders who conquered Jerusalem in 1099.

In the 19th century, the Crusades were understood, in America, within confessional frameworks: either regrettable but avoidable wars if a scholar was Catholic or a vicious demonstration of religious intolerance if a historian was Protestant. Of course, the Romanticism associated with the novels of Sir Walter Scott subsumed both confessional viewpoints within a popular medievalism of dashing knights, pious ladies and noble Muslims. Among scholars, such confessionalism, while never disappearing, was less explicit, especially after 1850 when German scientific methods of historical research were adopted in the United States. For instance, the great historian of the inquisition, Henry Charles Lea, writing in the 1880s and 1890s, viewed the Crusades, and not just the Albigensian, as evidence of the lack of tolerance he associated with the medieval Church. As American historians transformed the *Objektivität* associated with Leopold von Ranke into the 'objective science' of history between 1880 and 1930, religion was considered a topic inappropriate for historians. What interested Dana Munro, Austin Evans and Joseph Strayer – all of whom produced remarkable scholarship on the Crusades – were the institutional and legal aspects of crusading and not the religious aspects. This institutional perspective on the Crusades remains pervasive among American scholars. It should be noted that Mark Twain's *A Connecticut Yankee in King Arthur's Court* (1889), while not explicitly about the Crusades, was in part a satire of Scott's Romantic Middle Ages, which he thought deluded Southerners in the Civil War into thinking they were knights fighting a noble Crusade against the North.

In the aftermath of the First World War, the overt recognition by Americans that they were now a world power led many to see the United States as the protector and culmination of Western civilization. The 'manifest destiny' that justified American expansion beyond the Mississippi River to the Pacific Ocean in the 19th century was allied to the belief that America and not Europe was the destiny of the West in the 20th century. More than the Greeks or the Romans, this civilization was defined by the European Middle Ages. Charles Homer Haskins, in his *The Renaissance of the Twelfth Century* (1927), explicitly makes this point. (Haskins was also the first to establish university courses on Western civilization, which remain a staple of the American curriculum.) In Cecil B. DeMille's movie, *The Crusades* (1935), the villains were devious German nobles forsaking Western values of honour and piety, as opposed to Saladin and his warriors, who recognized religious virtues. During and after the Second World War, this ideal of defending Western civilization, whether against the Axis powers or the Soviet Union, was explicitly framed as an ongoing Crusade. For example, *Crusade in Europe* (1948) was the title of Dwight D. Eisenhower's memoir as Supreme Commander of the Allied Expeditionary Forces from 1944 to 1945. During the civil rights struggles of the 1960s, the idea that racial equality and justice was a Crusade worth fighting for – and even dying for – was widespread, as famously witnessed in the Birmingham Children's Crusade of 1963.

Among western democracies, the United States is unusual in being deeply religious, and mostly Christian, despite the constitutional separation of Church and State. In the latter half of the 20th century, any social movement with a clear moral purpose, especially one fulfilling the promise or destiny of America, was frequently named a 'Crusade'. In this sense, what was being evoked in the Crusades was a Christian idealistic 'city on the hill' – worth fighting for politically, socially and culturally, rather than militarily. This changed after the fall of the Soviet Union in 1989 and the New York terrorist attacks in 2001. Among scholars, the study of the Crusades remains important; among readers, it is immensely popular. Yet, in both cases, the religious dimension of holy war remains poorly understood. There is renewed interest inside and out of the academy about the question of religion, especially in Western countries where religion seemed to be an issue of the past. This interest has been powerfully spurred by terrorist attacks – domestic and foreign. All citizens within Western democracies now experience, even if at a distance, the consequences of religious violence, and so, more than ever, analysis of the medieval Crusades has never been more vital.

Literature

Henry Charles, L. *A History of the Inquisition*, 3 vols. New York, 1888.

Munro, D. C. 'War and History', *American Historical Review*, 32 (1927), pp. 219–231.

Strayer, J. *The Albigensian Crusades.* New York Press, 1971.

3.22 From Grunwald to Vienna – a view from Poland

Karol Polejowski

The Polish perception of the phenomenon of the Crusades in the Middle Ages (in Polish: *krucjaty* or *wyprawy krzyżowe*) was largely shaped in the 19th and 20th centuries through the prism of the presence of the Teutonic Order in the region of the Baltic Sea.[21] This religious military order, originally from the Holy Land, was invited to the Polish-Prussian borderland in the years 1226–1230. As a result of the systematic conquest of the area inhabited by the Prussian tribes (up until 1283), at the beginning of the 14th century, the Order founded its own state. Also at the beginning of the 14th century, the Teutonic Knights engaged in a conflict with Poland (1308–1343). From that moment, the brothers of the Teutonic Order have been inextricably linked with the image of an aggressive, ruthless and treacherous enemy of the Polish benefactors. From the period of the Polish-Teutonic wars, the Battle of Grunwald/Tannenberg 1410 remains the most famous and still holds an important place in Polish schoolbooks. The victory of the Polish-Lithuanian forces proved to be one of the most important events in Polish history and played an important role in the process of the creation of a Polish national consciousness in the Modern Era.

The specific character of the Polish-Teutonic Order was revealed in the 19th century, when the young German nationalism identified the Catholic Teutonic Order with the German civilizing mission and German 'Drang nach Osten' (Drive to the East). This became particularly evident after the partition of Poland (1772–1795), when the Prussian State absorbed a large part of Polish territories, including Malbork. The Castle of Malbork became one of the symbols of 'German civilisation' in the East, which defended the West from Slavic, that is, 'barbarian' expansion.

The Polish historians reacted to these developments by creating an image of the Teutonic Order as an 'eternal' enemy of Poland, which gave birth to the Prussian-German imperialism. This situation lasted until around the turn of the 20th century. The symbols linked with the Teutonic Order (white coat with the black cross) were used in the propaganda by the Germans, especially politicians and by the countries 'touched' by Teutonic Order aggression, including the Polish communist regime. It should be noted, however, that in the 1980s, the process of rapprochement of the Teutonic Order by Polish and German historians began. One of the results of this situation was the 'Ordines Militares' (organized in Toruń) conference, which became an important event for historians of the Middle Ages.

The collapse of communism (1989/1991) and the opening of the borders created a situation where Polish historians could take up the study of this phenomenon more broadly.

From the historiographical point of view, the Polish research on the Crusades can be divided into several areas. The first field of interest is the Polish participation in the Crusades in the 12th century, especially in the Second and Third Crusade, as well as the pilgrimage to the Holy Land in the second half of this century. But Polish participation in the Levantine Crusades was rather symbolic. In the 12th century, the most famous Polish crusader was Duke Henry of Sandomierz, who fought in the Holy Land in 1154–1155, and was killed during the expedition against the Prussian tribes in 1166. The next field of research concerns the 13th-century Crusades against the Mongol expansion in Eastern Europe. Another field of interest is connected with the participation of Polish knights in the Crusades in the 14th and 15th centuries, especially against Ottoman Turks. A rather small group of historians research the history of the Crusades in their European and Mediterranean aspects. A different field of research concerns the role of the Kingdom of Poland and the Polish-Lithuanian Commonwealth as the *Bulwark of Christianity*, especially in the 16th and 17th centuries. The Battle of Vienna (1683) has similar significance as the Battle of Grunwald.

The Crusades and Teutonic Order were present in Polish culture for at least two centuries. The most famous Polish poet, Adam Mickiewicz, wrote some poems, concerning the Teutonic Order. Henryk Sienkiewicz created a novel, *Krzyżacy (The Teutonic Knights)*, concerning the relations between Poland and Teutonic Order at the beginning of the 15th century. Also, the Battle of Grunwald was the theme of the most famous Polish painting *Bitwa pod Grunwaldem*, painted by Jan Matejko. In the 1960s, Aleksander Ford – one of the most famous Polish filmmakers – adapted the novel of Sienkiewicz and made one of the most popular Polish movies, *Krzyżacy (The Teutonic Knights)*. In the 1990s, after the collapse of communism, many Polish fans of medieval history created historical reconstruction groups. Till today, the most popular historical reconstructions are the Battle of Grunwald and the siege of Malbork, both events took place in 1410, during the war between the Kingdom of Poland and the Teutonic Order.

Literature

Biskup, M. and G. Labuda. *Dzieje zakonu krzyżackiego w Prusach: gospodarka, społeczeństwo, państwo, ideologia (History of the Teutonic Order in Prussia: Economy, Society, State, Ideology)*. Gdańsk, 1988.

Gładysz, M. *The Forgotten Crusaders: Poland and the Crusader Movement in the Twelfth and Thirteenth Centuries.* Leiden/ Boston, 2012.

Güttner-Sporzyński, D. von. *Poland, Holy War, and the Piast Monarchy, 1100–1230.* Turnhout, 2014.

Kowalska, Z. *Krzyżacy w innym świetle: od średniowiecza do czasów współczesnych (Teutonic Knights in a Different Light: From the Middle Ages to the Present Day].* Tarnów/Vienna, 1996.

Polejowski, K. *Wydawnictwo Naukowe Ateneum – Szkoły Wyższej w Gdańsku (Matrimonium et crux. The Briennne Family during the Crusades).* Gdańsk, 2014.

3.23 The Teutonic Order forgotten today – a view from Germany

Malte Prietzel

In the German-speaking historical research of the 19th and 20th centuries, the Crusades that made their way to the Near East between 1096 and 1291, were given little attention, as they did not fit nicely into the interpretative patterns of the 1960s which concentrated on national history .

However, a few researchers addressed the Crusades. Prior to the First World War, two academic outsiders – Reinhold Röhricht (1842–1905) and Heinrich Hagenmeyer (1834–1915) – wrote on the history of the Crusades and the crusader states. Their works remain essential: Röhricht's books made large amounts of materials available for research, while Hagenmeyer created editions rich in commentary. In 1935, Carl Erdmann's foundational work, *The Origins of the Idea of Crusading*, was published; his methodological approach was revolutionary not only within research on the Crusades. Erdmann was not interested in events and actions. Instead, he inquired into the development of a notion, namely that a war for the Christian faith could be religiously commendable. Since the 1960s, Hans Eberhard Mayer (*1932) has developed foundational studies that have also been recognised internationally. His research applied particularly to the political structures of the crusader states.

In the last two decades, German language research has engaged significantly more with the Crusades. The external impulse was the political events following the attacks on 9/11, 2001, and a considerably heightened interest in the Middle East and Islam. However, the turn towards researching the Crusades was also the result of a tendency in the humanities, namely, the openness to look to cultures outside of Europe. In fact, the recent German language contributions on the topic of the Crusades in the Near East are connected to research on the Mediterranean region, both personally and organizationally. Thus, the Crusades no longer appear as an exotic aspect of European history, but as pieces of wide-ranging interactions between cultures and religions.

Between 1860 and 1945, German historians and the German public gave much attention to the Crusades of the Teutonic Order against the 'heathen' Prussians in the south-eastern edge of the Baltic Sea, where the Order had founded its own state. Initially, this state was just considered as a part of the history of the then German provinces of East and West Prussia. Yet, the history of the State of the Teutonic

Order was soon distorted. In this view, the religious aspects barely played any role. It was much more about the idols of the late 19th century: the nation and the race. The main responsible for this change was Heinrich von Treitschke (1834–1896), a wild nationalist and racist, yet unfortunately highly gifted both stylistically and rhetorically. He influenced the German view of history more strongly than any other German historian of his time. For him, the expansion of the Teutonic Order was a civilizing act. He consciously appropriated the perspective of 19th-century colonialism when writing about the 13th-century Baltic Sea coast. For example, he spoke of 'German colonies' when he referred to towns founded or co-founded by German merchants, and he described the Prussians and their culture in a derogatory manner, just as others wrote at the same time about sub-Saharan Africa.

Treitschke wrote in a very similar way about the Polish. The Teutonic Order waged many wars against Poland in the 14th and 15th centuries and as a result, the Polish kings had subjects who spoke German. Many Germans of the late 19th and early 20th centuries saw this as intolerable. None of the medieval conflicts between the Order and Poland was a Crusade, as the Polish had been Christianized for a long time. However, in the disputes of the 19th century, the popular ideas of the Crusades – both the negative and the positive connotations – played a significant role. For Treitschke, the wars of the Teutonic Order against Poland were campaigns for civilization: secularised Crusades, if you will. Polish historians and novelists often called the Teutonic Knights 'crusaders' and described them as brutal conquerors.

This pattern of interpretation defined the historiography of both nations for a long time. Yet since the 1970s, a dynamic collaboration between German and Polish historians on the Teutonic Order has taken place, based on conferences organised at the university at Toruń, titled *Ordines militares*. Today, the Teutonic order does not play a role outside of the circle of historians and those interested in history, and in general, the former eastern provinces have disappeared from the German historical consciousness. The Teutonic Order still exists, but purely as a charitable organization.

Like the wars of the Teutonic Order, the Crusades in the Near East were interpreted with the help of anachronism in school books, popular books and novels. Additionally, today there is a strong interest in many ideas that connect to the word 'Crusade', but this does not concern the 'real' Crusades. Rather, this is a phenomenon of Anglo-American-influenced popular culture. In January 2019, the German website for the online shop Amazon listed more than 2000 books that had 'Crusades' or 'Crusade' in the title: academic books, popular science books and historical novels, but even more fantasy novels, books concerning computer games (whose scenarios have something to do with a 'Crusade') and books on contemporary subjects. Thus, there are books such as *Ratzinger and his Crusade* (about the alleged aspirations of Pope Benedict XV), books on the 'Islamic Crusade' (Jihad), and on the 'Crusade' to save the elephants. Myth is more interesting and powerful than the past.

Literature

Boockmann, H. *Der Deutsche Orden. Zwölf Kapitel aus seiner Geschichte (The Teutonic Order. Twelve Chapters from its History)*, Munich, 1981.

Erdmann, C. *Die Entstehung des Kreuzzugsgedankens (The Origin of the Idea of Crusading)*. Berlin, 1935.

Jaspert, N. *Die Kreuzzüge (The Crusades)* (Geschichte Kompakt). Darmstadt, 2003.

Mayer, H. E. *Geschichte der Kreuzzüge (History of the Crusades)*. Stuttgart, 2005.

Treitschke, H. von. ‚Das deutsche Ordensland Preußen' (The German Order Land of Prussia). *Preußische Jahrbücher* 10 (1862), pp. 95–151.

3.24 Constantinople pillaged, Venice risen and *Gerusalemme Liberata* – a view from Italy

Luigi Russo

A long-consolidated Italian historiographic tradition has relegated the history of the Crusades to a secondary chapter of the history of medieval Italy. Due to this situation – aside from some individual scholars – Italian academic research has basically ignored the study of the Crusades. It is often considered uninteresting for the history of the Italian peninsula, or is appraised as a chapter in the commercial expansion of the Italian communes in the Middle East (e.g. Venice, Genoa, Pisa and Amalfi) after the birth of the Latin Holy Land.

Despite this, it would be enough to cite a bull emitted by Pope Eugene III in the spring of 1146 – after the fall of Edessa into Muslim hands – to understand how relevant the contribution of the Italian population was for the success of the crusading movement ever since the 12th century. Recalling the events of the expedition that led to the conquest of Jerusalem in 1099, Eugene III recalled that "At his voice (*scil.* by Urban II), indeed, those beyond the mountain and especially the bravest and strongest warriors of the French kingdom [= Francorum regni],[22] and also those of Italy [= et illi etiam de Italia], inflamed by the ardour of love, did come together" (transl. from E.F. Henderson, *Select Historical Documents of the Middle Ages*, New York 1965, p. 334). The pivotal role of Venice in the crusading expedition that led to the plundering of Constantinople in the years 1203–1204[23] should also be noted, as well as the influence of the Italian humanists during the events of the Ottoman expansion, culminating in the conquest of the Byzantine capital in 1453, which put an end to the millennial history of the Eastern Roman Empire (better known as Byzantine Empire). The latter provided a global interpretative paradigm for interpreting the ongoing clash with the Turkish world.[24] Viewing the Turkish world as barbarian was destined to influence the historiography of the Crusades.

The Italian contribution to the Crusades was also present in literature. An example of this can be found in the *Gerusalemme liberata* by Torquato Tasso (1544–1595), a poet born in Sorrento – near Naples – focusing on the exploits of the knights who conquered Jerusalem during the so-called 'First Crusade'. Published in 1581, the epic-religious poem of Tasso became one of the texts intended to significantly influence the perception of the Crusade events in European public opinion. It was almost immediately translated and read across Europe, up until the time of Walter Scott. Moreover, Tasso's text is still included in Italian secondary schools curricula, and is, therefore, studied every year by thousands of Italian students. This reveals its enduring influence.

Clearly, the vicissitudes of the Crusades had vivid repercussions in the Italian peninsula, a heritage that the most recent historiography has just begun to emphasize with greater attention. An example of this is in the legends created during the Late Middle Ages in numerous Italian cities (Florence and Milan are the most famous ones) about the presence of their compatriots who first entered the Holy City after the victorious siege in 1099. This testifies the strong wish of a large number of city-communities to link their own histories to the crusading movement in a substantial reformulation of their past, a topic that deserves – in my opinion – further study.

Nevertheless, the minor interest in the history of the Crusades related to the events of Italian history remains undeniable. This is evidenced by the number of quotations available on the web analysed in a recent study conducted by Antonio Brusa. The study highlighted the minor presence of the word '*crociata*' (Crusade) comparing it with the occurrences in analogous Spanish and English websites.

On the other hand, to conclude, it should be noted that the tragic events of 9/11 have also reoriented the Italian public opinion on the debate about the origins of the worldwide clash between Christianity and Islam. The topic remains hotly debated in parallel with the increasing presence of Muslims in Italy – today amounting to 3.7% of the total population (PEW Research Center Data).[25] This represents a challenge (also cultural) that the Italian intellectual and academic world will have to take up and develop in the coming decades.

Literature

AA.VV. *Gli Italiani e la Terrasanta (The Italians and the Holy Land)*, ed. A. Musarra. Florence, 2014.

Brusa, A. 'Internet e la rete degli stereotipi sul Medioevo' (Internet and the Network of Stereotypes about the Middle Ages). In *«Apprendere ciò che vive». Studi offerti a Raffaele Licinio*, ed. F. Violante and V. Rivera Magos. Bari, 2017, pp. 85–118.

Cardini, F. *In Terrasanta. Pellegrini italiani tra Medioevo e prima età moderna (In the Holy Land. Italian Pilgrims Between the Middle Ages and the Early Modern Age)*. Bologna, 2002.

Meserve, M. 'Italian Humanists and the Problem of the Crusade'. In *Crusading in the Fifteenth Century*, ed. N. Housley. Basingstoke, 2004, pp. 13–38.

Russo, L. I. *Normanni del Mezzogiorno e il movimento crociato (The Normans of the South and the Crusader Movement)*. Bari, 2014, pp. 7–20.

Siberry, E. 'Tasso and the Crusades. History of a legacy', *Journal of Medieval History* XIX (1993), pp. 163–169.

3.25 700 years of slavery – a view from Estonia

Anti Selart

The Estonian view of the Crusades (*ristisõda* – 'War of the Cross') is unequivocally linked with the Baltic Crusades. The Crusades in the Medeiterranean were, and continue to be, in Estonian language mainly represented by translations – both in non-fiction and fiction. This topic has only been addressed in a few original books by authors Karl Ristikivi (1912–1977) and Tiit Aleksejev (1968).

The Estonian national concept of history that arose in the second half of the 19th century fundamentally rests on Enlightenment thought and anticlerical social criticism that emerged around 1800. The main representative of this criticism was the Baltic-German writer Garlieb Merkel (1769–1850). This view of history brought about a sharp juxtaposition. On the one hand, there was the fortunate, and more or less democratic prehistory, and on the other hand, a vicious and bloody subjugation by conquerors. The conquerors were viewed as having brought the Estonians enslavement and bondage: the 'Seven Hundred Year Slavery'. At the same time, this view was a distinctly Lutheran one. For instance, whenever the spiritual aspects of the Crusades were mentioned, it was only in a negative context. Indulgences and Baptism were regarded as ideological concealment of the bloody deeds perpetrated by Catholic robber barons and murderers. Since the Catholics themselves – with their power-hungry and greedy Pope at the top – did not know true Christian faith, the Christianization 'with fire and sword' was bound to remain only the appearance of true baptism.

Like German authors, the Estonians perceived the Baltic Crusades primarily as German expansion. Thus, in the Middle Ages, Livonia was a (German) colony. Insofar as the Germans saw these incidents as part of their historical and civilizing obligation, the Estonians considered the Germans an archenemy and *the* entire source of the historical misfortunes of Estonia.[26] Generally speaking, in the 1920s, this conception of events was taken up by the emerging Estonian academic historiography. In the 1930s, the concept of 'Muistne vabadusvõitlus' (the 'ancient' or 'historical fight for freedom') gained acceptance. This concept connected the lost battle in the 13th century and the victorious Estonian War of Independence from 1918 to 1920. This view held that the freedom which was lost in the Middle Ages was now chiefly understood as political autonomy. It was anchored in the popular consciousness by historical fiction. One example of this can be found in the novel 'Ümera jõel' ('*At the Ümera river*') (1934) by Mait Metsanurk (1879–1957), which was about the Estonian victory against the German knights.

Due to the resistance to soviet Russian-centric and often coarsely Marxist historiography – which was violently imposed – the image of the nation from the 1930s was effectively conserved. The soviet occupation from 1944 to 1991 also brought about difficulties in communication. In many respects, at this time Estonian historical scholarship was isolated from the new developments in international historiography. But concurrently, Estonian culture's historically anti-German disposition fell out of fashion. Furthermore, Estonia's strong bond with Western Europe brought about by the Crusades became increasingly perceived as a positive aspect of the conquest.

Since the turn of the century, the so-called pluralistic approach to the Baltic Crusades became the standard approach in Estonian academic historiography. They see the Crusades as a part of the entire European history of the Crusades. Instead of a German-Estonian war, it is rather described as a complex occurrence, wherein neither of the two 'camps' were unified.

Yet in public discourse – exemplified by the public dicussion after the publication of a new general history of Estonia's Middle Ages – the national and romantic concept of Estonia's history still dominates. This is also received as an aspect of the Estonian national identity. Currently, the public view of the Crusades in the Mediterranean region is increasingly influenced by the discourses in English and their translations.

Literature

Jensen, C. S. 'Appropriating history: Remembering the Crusades in Latvia and Estonia'. In *Rememebering the Crusades and Crusading*, ed. Megan Cassidy-Welch, London, 2017, pp. 231–246.

Kala, T., L. Kaljundi, J. Kreem et al. *Eesti ajalugu II: Eesti keskaeg (History of Estonia II: Estonian Middle Ages)*. Tartu, 2012.

Kaljundi, L. 'The Chronicler and the Modern World. Henry of Livonia and the Baltic Crusades in the Enlightenment and National Traditions'. In *Crusading and Chronicle Writing on the Medieval Baltic Frontier*, ed. Marek Tamm, Linda Kaljundi, Carsten Selch Jensen. Farnham, 2011, pp. 409–455.

Selart, A., 'Historical Legitimacy and Crusade in Livonia'. In *Crusading on the Edge. Ideas and Practice of Crusading in Iberia and the Baltic Region, 1100–1500*, ed. Torben K. Nielsen and Iben Fonnesberg-Schmidt. Turnhout, 2016, pp. 29–54.

Vahtre, S. *Muinasaja loojang Eestis. Vabadusvõitlus, 1208–1227 (The Final Phase of Prehistory in Estonia. The Fight for Freedom, 1208–1227)*. Tallinn, 1990.

3.26 The axe of Lalli and the cap of St. Henry – a view from Finland

Miikka Tamminen

The Crusades have traditionally played an important role in Finnish historiography. In Finland, the focus has been on the so-called Northern Crusades or the Swedish Crusades to Finland.[27] The Crusade campaigns to the Holy Land and to other regions have not received the same amount of attention.

The Finnish term for Crusade is *ristiretki*, which is a compound of words *risti*, meaning 'the cross', and *retki*, meaning 'an expedition'. The term thus roughly translates as 'the cross expedition'. The Finnish *ristiretki* is a similar term to *korståg* in Swedish and *Kreuzzug* in German, all pointing univocally to both the spiritual and the military sides of crusading.

The medieval period ranging from 1150 to 1350 has traditionally been labelled as 'the Period of the Crusades' in Finland. This period has further been divided into episodes of three major Crusades: the so-called First Crusade to Finland, normally dated to the 1150s, specifically the year 1155; the Second Crusade to central Finland against the Tavastians, which is dated to 1238–39, sometimes to 1249; and the Third Crusade against the Karelians in 1293. The sources for the first two Crusades are scarce and written much later than the alleged expeditions took place. The debate among scholars has mainly focused on the dating of these Crusades.

The 'Period of the Crusades' has often been viewed from two distinct perspectives. Both of these perspectives were influenced by medieval legends and later historical events. On the one hand, the Crusades to Finland have been regarded as Swedish attempts to conquer the land. The Finnish-speaking people living in the region have been viewed as the victims of these military campaigns. On the other hand, the Swedish crusaders have been interpreted as Christian soldiers who introduced Western values and brought Christianity to Finland.

The latter perspective has placed the Swedish crusaders and the Finns ultimately on the same side in the historiography of the Crusades. The Swedes and the Finns fought together as allies against the common enemy in the East, the Novgorodians or the Russians.[28] The medieval Crusades were a prelude to the later centuries of warfare fought along the Eastern border. During the Second World War, this historic tradition was actively utilized by the Finnish army. Furthermore, the war against the Soviet Union was presented as another

Crusade against the old enemy. The Finnish Lutheran clergy sought to demonstrate, particularly during the Continuation War of 1941–44, that the war against the Soviets was 'a holy Crusade' in defence of the true faith.

The most famous figures of the Crusades to Finland are those from the so-called First Crusade. This expedition was allegedly made by King Eric of Sweden and Bishop Henry. The history of this Crusade abounds with myths and uncertainties. The campaign may have simply been a raid, which was later described a Crusade, if it ever existed at all. After the expedition, Bishop Henry is said to have died as a martyr at the hands of a native Finn. A vernacular poem, known as the *surmavirsi*, later identified the killer as a man named Lalli.

The roots of the *Piispa Henrikin surmavirsi* (the Ballad of the death of Bishop Henry) originate in folklore and possibly go as far back as the late 13th or early 14th century. The first written accounts of the poem are from the 17th century. Lalli is described in the poem as a peasant from Köyliö, who in anger killed the visiting bishop with an axe on the nearby frozen lake. Lalli then took the bishop's cap, put it on his head and went home. There, he took the cap off, but by the judgement of God, all his hair and scalp came off as well. This and many other miracles performed by the dead crusading bishop are told in the poem and the hagiographic *Legenda sancti Henrici* from the late 13th century.

Both the deceased bishop and his killer became important figures in the making of the 'Finnish identity' during the premodern and the modern eras. The veneration of St. Henry helped consolidate the position of the Catholic Church in the region. Henry became the patron saint of Finland, whose relics were even visited from afar. Lalli became the arch-villain, the enemy of the crusaders and all the civilized Christians in Finland: "the worst of all the pagans, the cruellest in the midst of all the Judases", in the words of the *surmavirsi*. However, later nationalistic history writing regarded Lalli also as the first Finn, who rose against oppression and fought against the taxation of the Church.

In recent studies, the tenability of the accounts describing the First Crusade and the historicity of both Henry and Lalli has been questioned. Curiously, this has provoked an outcry from the Finnish public and debate, where the historical existence of Henry and Lalli has been defended. In present-day, secular Finnish society, the martyrdom of Henry still appears to have great relevance. St. Henry is a celebrated figure in both the Lutheran and the Catholic churches of Finland. His place of death is visited annually by pilgrims. Lalli has a statue of his own in Köyliö, and he was even voted the 14th greatest Finn of all time in a poll held in Finland in 2004.

Literature

Heikkilä, T. *Pyhän Henrikin legenda (The Legend of St Henry)*. Helsinki, 2006.

Lehtonen, T. M. S. and K. Villads Jensen (eds.) *Medieval History Writing and Crusading Ideology*. Tampere, 2005.

Tilli, J. *Suomen pyhä sota (The Holy War of Finland)*. Jyväskylä, 2014.

Topelius, Z. *Maamme kirja (Book of Our Land)*. Helsinki, 1875.

3.27 The Crusaders as allies – a view from Georgia

Mamuka Tsurtsumia

"At this time came the Franks and captured Jerusalem and Antioch, and with the help of God recovered the land of Kartli and David gained more power and gathered his forces and stopped to pay tribute to the Sultan and the Turks were unable to spend the winters in Kartli anymore". This sentence connects the history of Georgia to the prominent movement known as the Crusades, which started in Clermont with the sermon of Urban II in 1095 and was followed by the taking of Jerusalem in 1099. The extract quoted earlier, taken from the ancient historical chronicles *The Life of Kartli*, directly connects the success of the greatest king of Georgia, David IV (1089–1125), to the First Crusade. It also proved to be defining in regard to the attitude of Georgian society towards the Crusades. It is true that the crusaders were only mentioned a few times in Georgian chronicles, where they are referred as Franks. The modern Georgian term *jvarosani* is a later introduction and literally means 'cross bearer'. Despite this fact, the results of the First Crusade have always been remembered in Georgia, specifically in scholarly circles.

Georgian historiography of the 20th century revealed considerable interest in the Crusades. However, the research was mainly confined to the study of the relationships between Georgia and the crusader states.

The approach to the issue in question by Georgian historians can be characterized by two main features. On the one hand, they looked at the Crusades from an extremely materialistic point of view; by doing so, they paid tribute to the opinions that persisted in Soviet historiography regarding the causes and reasons for the Crusades.[29] Specifically, they considered the Crusades a movement of the landless younger sons of feudal families seeking land and riches. And all this was organized by the Catholic Church, which had sent knights, greedy for loot and land, to the East. According to them, during these predatory wars, the true goals of the Crusades were revealed. The fanatical religious wars, accompanied by ruthless murders and looting, were considered a military-political adventure. In all fairness, it should also be mentioned that a well-known work published overseas by a Georgian emigrant, Zurab Avalishvili, defined the materialistic assessment of the Crusades. He conjectured that the goal of invading the Eastern lands, gaining control of trade and maritime roads, was preconceived.

On the other hand, as indicated by almost all Georgian historians, the Crusades carry great importance for Georgia's struggle against Seljuk Turks.[30] After the arrival of the crusaders, Georgia was not left on its own against the Seljuks. Therefore, the Crusades had a genuinely positive impact on the successful outcome of the Georgian battle for freedom. Georgian historiography always points out the participation of the Franks in the Battle of Didgori (1121), which established Georgian precedence in the region for a long time. Additionally, they draw attention to the mutual respect between Georgians and crusaders and their joint plans against Muslims. Furthermore, the correspondence between Pope Honorius III and Queen Rusudan reveals that in 1223 Georgians took up the cross and were ready to join the Crusade that had been planned. In addition, Georgian historians emphasized the significance of the Crusades for establishing contact between East and West and for developing international trade and maritime ties.

For contemporary Georgian historians, it is also clear that the Crusades, which dominated European thought for more than four centuries, were a much more complex phenomenon and that the motivation of the crusaders was less materialistic than portrayed.

Overall, unless the focus is placed on Soviet clichés, Georgian historiography assesses the Crusades positively, accepting the objective, positive contribution in the process of the liberation of Georgia from the Seljuk rule. Modern Georgian historiography also shares these assessments of their predecessors. Moreover, several historians, often without source proof evidence, make an attempt to find an analogy of the crusader movement in the history of Georgia. Though the issue of holy wars is yet to be studied in our historiography, one can say definitely that Georgian Christianity was endowed with a militant spirit. Like Europeans, the Georgian priesthood did not avoid fighting in the war. Military actions of the clergymen did not evoke the negative attitude as it did in Byzantium. It can be argued that Christian Georgia contradicted Muslim jihad with the war for 'Christ's faith'. Although it might appear like the conception of the holy war in Latin Christendom, it would be an exaggeration to label this as a crusader movement.

Finally, while evaluating attitudes of modern Georgian society towards the Crusades, they should be classified as more or less positive. The most obvious expression of this benevolent attitude is the fact that the nickname of the Georgian national team in football and basketball is the *Crusaders*.

Georgian literature also paid its debt to these tendencies, producing several historical novels where crusaders are portrayed positively, which undoubtedly reflects the views of society in general. This is also true of the recently published novel by D. Turashvili, which once again points out that the Crusades still remain an important historical subject for contemporary Georgian society.

Literature

Avalishvili, Z. *Jvarosanta droidan (From the Time of the Crusaders)*. Paris, 1929.

Badridze, S. *Sakartvelo da jvarosnebi (Georgia and the Crusaders)*. Tbilisi, 1973.

Meskhia, S. *Dzlevai sakvirveli (The Miraculous Victory)*. Tbilisi, 1972.

Metreveli, R. *Davit IV aghmashenebeli (David IV the Builder)*. Tbilisi, 1986.

Tsurtsumia, M. 'Pirveli jvarosnuli lashkroba da kartvelebi' (The First Crusade and the Georgians). In *Macne, Proceedings of the Georgian National Academy of Sciences* 1 (2017).

Selected popular items:

Gamsakhurdia, Konstantine. *Davit aghmashenebeli (David the Builder)*, 4 vols. Tbilisi, 1946–1958.

Turashvili, Dato. *Tkeebis mefe (The King of the Woods)*. Tbilisi, 2013.

Notes

1 See article of Pegg in this book.
2 See articles of Isa and Al-Zo'by in this book.
3 See articles of Chrissis and Coureas in this book.
4 See article of García-Guijarro Ramos in this book.
5 See article of Russo in this book.
6 See articles of Balard and Lobrichon in this book.
7 See article of Ersan in this book.
8 See article of García-Guijarro Ramos in this book.
9 See article of Hemptinne in this book.
10 See article of Russo in this book.
11 See article of Ersan in this book.
12 See article of Selart in this book.
13 See articles of Isa and Al Zo'by in this book.
14 See article of Selart in this book.
15 See article of Fonnesberg Schmidt in this book.
16 See article of Prietzel in this book.
17 See article of Tamminen in this book.
18 See also article of Balard from another French perspective in this book.
19 See article of El-Azhari in this book.
20 Remarks by the President Upon Arrival (Sept. 16, 2001): https://georgewbush-whitehouse.archives.gov/news/releases/2001/09/20010916-2.html (25.05.2019).

21 See article of Prietzel in this book.
22 See articles of Balard, Lobrichon, Hemptinne, Van Moolenbroek and Prietzel in this book.
23 See article of Chrissis in this book.
24 See article of Ersan in this book.
25 Source: www.pewresearch.org/fact-tank/2016/07/19/5-facts-about-the-muslim-population-in-europe/
26 See article of Prietzel in this book.
27 See article of Villads Jensen in this book.
28 See article of Bagdasarjan in this book.
29 See article from Ernestovich Bagdasarjan in this book.
30 See article from Ersan in this book.

4 First interpretations of the case studies

Felix Hinz and Johannes Meyer-Hamme

When comparing the contributions, it becomes immediately apparent that the approaches, perspectives and priorities of the authors are extremely diverse. Even though all of them used the concept of 'Crusades' in relation to the respective historical culture, even as a metaphor, it is striking that they understood the term quite differently. In the following, the texts on the history of the Crusades will be examined regarding the four aspects which were established from historical theory as presented in ch. 2. This is based on a qualitative analysis of the content.[1]

1 To what extent are the interests and functions of the narrative about the history of the Crusades identifiable for the present?
2 Which concepts and forms of historical interpretation are available?
3 Which concrete references to the past[2] are selected and mentioned?
4 To what degree can the descriptions of the historical cultures be characterized by one of the different dimensions of historical cultures?

1. To what extent are the interests and functions of the narrative of the history of the Crusades identifiable for the present?

Each story is told in the context of a specific present, and is consequently the expression of the orientation needs of that present. This also applies to the texts at hand. When we turn to the question of the present, it must first be determined which present is being considered. On the one hand, all the authors write from out of their own present. (The majority of the texts were written in 2016). However, in their contributions, they reference different meanings of the Crusades that arose in past times. In many cases, the authors mention, when appropriate, that the Crusades were of great importance in a rather recent past for the group whose perspective is being written about; yet, that is no longer the case, or even the other way around. In addition, the foci may have spectacularly shifted within a few decades due to decisive events. For example, this can be observed within the historical culture of Germany: While the history of the Crusades in the Baltics played an especially important part for the national-socialist ideology in the conquest in Eastern Europe, its importance decreased massively in the public historical culture following the end of the Second World War and the loss of the German eastern territories. Due to the political opposition between West and East Germany, they developed differing points of inquiry regarding the history of the Crusades. Ever since the attacks of 9/11, the history of the Crusades suddenly became relevant again, but with the focus on Jerusalem (cf. Prietzel).

Looking at the frequently mentioned past when the history of the Crusades was relevant, a pattern becomes clear: the Crusades were especially important in connection to nation building. This not only applies to Europe, but evidently for the Arabic historical cultures as well.

Applying the Crusades in this manner can certainly be interpreted under the perspective of 'invented traditions' (Hobsbawm/Ranger 1983). Above all, they point out the social functions of historical narratives and how previously non-existent states were provided with a myth of origin. An instance of this can be clearly seen in the contribution of García-Guijarro Ramos (Spain portrayed as the result of a successful crusading character of the reconquista against the Arabs) or in Hemptinne's contribution (Godfrey of Bouillon as a national hero, or ostensibly the 'first Belgian' on the world stage).

These national patterns of origin prove to be widespread. The only exceptions among our contributors are the historical cultures of Greece, Ireland, Italy and the Netherlands. According to Chrissis, the Byzantine Empire – "traditionally seen as the 'Medieval Greek Empire'" – is interpreted as a victim of the Crusades or the Roman Catholic Church. Therefore, an antagonism can be seen that is not only directed at Islam (considered 'Turkish'), but also towards Roman Catholic Christianity (cf. also Coureas on Cyprus besides Chrissis).

In general, it is clear from the contributions that the Crusades were viewed positively in times of imperialism as future-oriented founding myths. Conversely, in the historical cultures of post-colonial and democratic countries, the Crusades are viewed rather critically. A positive identification of the Crusades – apart from the special cases of Malta and Georgia – is virtually only located in the ultra-right milieu (i.e. in the national 'defence leagues') and that of right-wing terrorism, like what took place on the Norwegian island Utøya (cf. Aavitsland) in 2011.[3]

In the Maltese historical culture, according to Buttigieg, the romance of the Knights Hospitaller is marketed to tourists, as the nation is a former religious state with a successful war history against Islam. In the historical culture of Georgia, the history of the Crusades is given a positive interpretation as it is told as the history of the alleviation from the oppression of the Seljuks.

Conversely, the contribution on the historical culture of Syria makes it clear that the commonly longed-for goal of a unified 'Arabic' state or empire remains – with the belief that it would be able to better assert its own interests against the West. The blame for this state not existing today is not placed upon the respective societies and governments in the region. Instead, the blame is placed, in a simplistic way, on the West – particularly on Western Europe. Saladin is a major figure who, alongside his triumph over the Christians, stands for Arabic unity. As a result, he plays a role in all the contributions from the Arabic world (cf. Isa, El-Azhari and Al-Zo'by).

In connection to this, it should be mentioned that a connection is repeatedly made between the history of the Crusades and colonialism (in particular, Isa on Syria, Bagdasarjan on Russia, Jensen on Sweden and Chrissis on Greece). Occasionally, today the Crusades are compared with religious fundamentalism (Russo on Italy) and actually Islamism. Van Moolenbroek even observes that in Dutch "newspapers and magazines, the former crusader states of the twelfth century have been compared more than once with the present-day 'IS' (Islamic State)".

There is not only a special and temporal *standpoint* that belongs to the perspective of a historical account, but also a *direction of view*. In many – but certainly not all – of the texts, the history of the Crusades is closely tied to the capture (or the 'liberation') of Jerusalem and the appeal of Pope Urban II in 1095 (cf. Table 4.1). In some of the texts, the Crusades to the Levant are mentioned alongside other Crusades. Therefore, the combined military activities will be presented here. The accounts of the historical cultures of Portugal and Spain provide an example of this (Costa and García-Guijarro Ramos). In these accounts, the history of the reconquista and the history of the discovery and conquest of the Americas are equally at least partially interpreted as crusades. Furthermore, in the historical culture of Estonia, the idea of the Crusades is extended from the resistance and fight for freedom against the German Crusaders to the opposition against the perceived occupation by the Soviet Union (cf. Selart). In some of the texts, Jerusalem and 'The Holy Land' are not mentioned at all (e.g. Tamminen on the historical culture of Finland). In other texts, a distinction between kinds or destinations of Crusades is explicitly made (e.g. Jensen on the historical culture of Sweden). A somewhat coarse summarization of the contributions yields the following 'regional narrative families'.

Table 4.1 Important dates of the Crusades mentioned in the articles

Date	*Event (just "conquest" = conquest by the Franks)*	*Turning point (if needed)*	*Author*	*Country*
638	Muslims conquered Jerusalem		Ersan	Turkey
1091	conquest of Malta		Buttigieg	Malta
1095	**Urban II's call for the First Crusade**	**Beginning of the Crusades**	Fonnesberg-Schmidt	Denmark
			Tsurtsumia	Georgia
			Menache	Israel
			van Moolenbroek	Netherlands
			Carvalho Pinto Costa	Portugal
			Ersan	Turkey
1096	**Beginning of the First Crusade**		Lobrichon	France
			Prietzel	Germany
			Ersan	Turkey
	Pogroms against Jews		Menache	Israel
1099	**Conquest of Jerusalem**	**Beginning of Frankish rule in Jerusalem**	Hemptinne	Belgium
			El-Azhari	Egypt
			Tsurtsumia	Georgia
			Russo	Italy
			van Moolenbroek	Netherlands
			Jensen	Sweden
			Pegg	USA
1101	Crusades of 1101 in Anatolia		Ersan	Turkey
1111	Norwegian king, Sigurd Magnusson, reaches the Holy Land		Aavitsland	Norway
1118	Conquest of Zaragoza (Spain)		García-Guijarro Ramos	Spain
1147	Pope Eugenius III authorized a campaign against the pagan Slavs		Fonnesberg-Schmidt	Denmark
	Conquest of Lisbon		Cavalho Pinto Costa	Portugal

(*continued*)

Date	*Event (just "conquest" = conquest by the Franks)*	*Turning point (if needed)*	*Author*	*Country*
1155	**First Swedish Crusade against Finland**	**Finland became part of the Occident**	Tamminen	Finland
			Jensen	Sweden
1187	**Battle of Hattin, Saladin conquers Jerusalem**	**End of Frankish rule in Jerusalem**	El-Azhari	Egypt
			van Moolenbroek	Netherlands
			Isa	Syria
1204	**Conquest of Constantinople**	"The Fourth Crusade […] is seen as a major turning point. Indeed, the interpretation of Byzantine-Latin interaction often gets entangled in the question of Modern Greece's place in the world, and particularly in Europe" (Chrissis).	Crissis	Greece
			Russo	Italy
1212	**Children's Crusade**		Hemptinne	Belgium
			van Moolenbroeck	Netherlands
1218	Crusaders conquer parts of the Nile-Delta		El-Azhari	Egypt
	Fifth Crusade conquers Damietta		van Moolenbroek	Netherlands
1219	The Danish King, Valdemar II, conquers parts of northern Estonia		Fonnesberg-Schmidt	Denmark
1223	'Georgians took up the cross and were ready to join the planned crusade'		Tsurtsurmia	Georgia

Date	Event (just "conquest" = conquest by the Franks)	Turning point (if needed)	Author	Country
1291	**Khalil conquers Acre**	**End of Frankish rule in the Holy Land**	El-Azhari	Egypt
			Prietzel	Germany
			Crissis	Greece
			Menache	Israel
			Isa	Syria
			Ersan	Turkey
1410	Battle of Grunwald/Tannenberg		Polejowski	Poland
1453	**Fall of Constantinople**	- "Ideal of the crusade flared up shortly" (Hemptinne)	Hemptinne	Belgium
		- "Ottoman expansion culminating in the conquest of the Byzantine capital" (Russo)	Russo	Italy
1492	Conquest of Granada		García-Guijarro Ramos	Spain
	Discovery of America	Since then "the Eastern Mediterranean, including Cyprus, steadily lost its importance to the West".	Coureas	Cyprus (Greek part)
1683	Second siege of Vienna		Polejowski	Poland
1798	Napoleon's departure to Egypt		Lobrichon	France
	"the forces of Revolutionary-Republican France, under Napoleon, ousted the Hospitallers from Malta" (Buttigieg)		Buttigieg	Malta
1917	General Allenby conquers Jerusalem		Horswell/Phillips	Great Britain
1920	General Henri Gouraud mocked the Arabs in Damascus		Isa	Syria

(*continued*)

Date	*Event (just "conquest" = conquest by the Franks)*	*Turning point (if needed)*	*Author*	*Country*
1963	Children's Crusade of 1963		Pegg	USA
1989/91	**Collapse of communism**		Polejowski Pegg	Poland USA
1991	**Estonia regained its independence**	Since then much political, economic and cultural collaboration between Denmark and Estonia	Fonnesberg-Schmidt Selart	Denmark Estonia
	American intervention in Iraq		Al-Zoby	Jordan
2001 (9/11)	**Terrorist attacks in the USA**	- Newly awakened interest in the Arabic region - "The tragic events of 9/11 have also reoriented the Italian public opinion on the debate about the origins of the worldwide clash between Christianity and Islam, a hotly debated topic in parallel with the increasing presence of Muslims in Italy" (Russo)	Prietzel Russo García-Guijarro Ramos Pegg	Germany Italy Spain USA
2004	Terrorist attacks in Madrid		García-Guijarro Ramos	Spain
2011	Norway suffered a terrorist attack from a right-wing extremist 'Templar'		Aavitsland	Norway

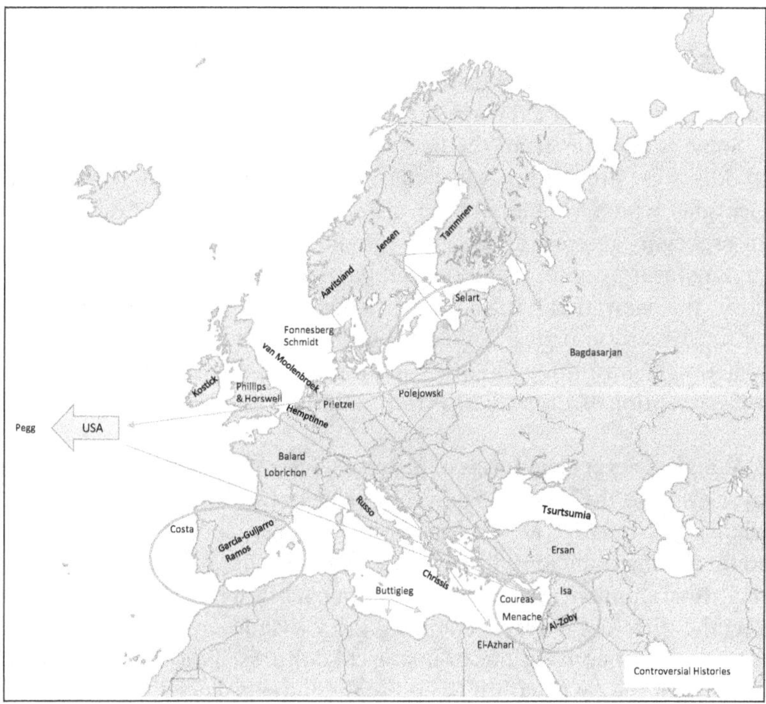

Map 4.1 References mentioned in the contributions and resulting "narrative families" of the crusade history

The destinations crystallize around three main areas:

a Jerusalem: To this day in the historical cultures of most countries of the formerly Christian West, the attention is almost exclusively placed upon Jerusalem when considering the subject, 'Crusades'.

b The Baltic States: In contrast, all of the historical cultures bordering the Baltic Sea focus exclusively on the east Baltic States, which were Christianized during the Middle Ages.

c The former Moorish Iberian Peninsula: In the historical cultures of Portugal and Spain, the interest is still today predominantly directed towards the Iberian Peninsula and North Africa. This is because they see themselves as successor states to those that invested their entire energy in the reconquista during the Middle Ages.

In this way, there is a large degree of overlap between the formation of 'narrative-families' and the historical crusading communities and defence alliances of the Crusades of the Middle Ages. This can be interpreted as a testament to the persistent potency of traditional perspectives and historical identity.

Some exceptions from the periphery of the West at the time of the Middle Ages are the historical cultures of Ireland, Malta, Turkey and Georgia, which should not be classified with others. Additionally, an especially interesting exception is the historical culture of Russia. In Bagdasarjan's contribution (similar to Chrissis' Greek contribution), the view that Orthodox Christianity is continually oppressed by the West dominates. This can be interpreted as a traditional construction of meaning. Although subliminal, Russia clearly possesses a self-perception as the successor to Byzantium.

2. Which concepts and forms of historical interpretation are available?

In relation to the concepts (see ch. 2), one naturally asks the question: what is a Crusade? Depending on the answer, certain undertakings count among them and, if they are considered significant, even receive their own number as the first, second or tenth Crusade. In this manner, the different ways of counting the Crusades come about. These also represent conventions of historical cultures. This is also reflected in some of the texts within the present volume. According to Tamminen, within the Finnish historical culture, the Swedish Crusades are dominant (three of which were addressed). Also, Tamminen explains that the war against the USSR was and remains a 'Crusade' for many Finns. Other contributions view entirely other subjects as activities considered 'Crusades'.[4]

In the texts on historical cultures, in connection with the theoretical premises, differing patterns of constructs of meaning are identifiable in the sense of Jörn Rüsen (see Chapter 2). In part, it is clear that in some historical cultures the interpretation prevails that the Crusades, as a phenomenon of the Middle Ages, have little importance for the present (e.g. in the historical culture of Italy). And if they do receive interpretation, then they are seen as something backwards. The form of this construct of meaning is based on the underlying premises of directional development, wherein the Crusades are unimportant for the present and the future. These cases have to do with an affirmative-genetic construct of meaning.

The Estonian historical culture presents another case, where, according to Selart, the Crusades are interpreted within the context of 'seven hundred years of slavery'. The Soviet era is included in this period. There are exemplary interpretative patterns here that assume small Estonia must be careful that it would not once again fall under foreign domination by an overpowering neighbour.

Traditional patterns of constructs of meaning are much more common. The contributions on the historical cultures of Syria and Jordan are evidence of the tendency towards tradition. They could be described more precisely, according to Körber, as affirmative-factual, in that they assume that the antagonism with the West existed since the beginning of the Crusades and, looking to the future, is simply a given (Isa on Syria and Al-Zo'by on Jordan). The experiences of the past will be protracted into the future. The history of the State of Israel is also included in this interpretation. Then again, this is "undoubtedly a mistake", in the opinion of Balard from a French perspective, "as there are no similarities between the ideology of the crusaders – who set off for the Holy Land to search for their salvation – and that of the Israelis, who primarily endeavour to settle in the land of their ancestors from the times of antiquity".

Likewise, the historical culture of Finland can be identified with a traditional construct of meaning (Tamminen). The dominant narrative here is that the Finns initially defended themselves against the invading Swedes. Yet ultimately the Christianization and Europeanization were viewed as something gained, rather than something that should be renounced. Thus, it becomes clear that traditional constructs of meaning can take entirely different forms.

An example demonstrating that the authors must in no way concur with the dominant narratives in the historical culture is represented by Isa. He worked under the Baath-Party as a history teacher in Syria but fled to Germany during the conflict there. Although he recites a view that is very familiar with the Baath-Party, he distances himself from the ideology. It is one of the cases in which the author makes explicit critical sense and places himself in a distanced relationship to the dominant interpretation of historical culture. This example shows that there are texts in this volume in which the authors do not write about their personal views, but about interpretations of the historical cultures that they consider dominant.

3. Which concrete references to the past are selected and mentioned?

The particular orientation needs, as well as the concepts and forms of historical interpretation, determine the selection of historical data and 'facts' that are referenced for the argument of the narrative. For every narration (regardless of scope), the narrator must always select, name and omit historical data. What is now required is simply to decide what should be seen as the beginning of the Crusades. It is already evident that no specific event can account for the Crusades. Alongside the frequently mentioned call of Pope Urban II in 1095 (e.g. Fonnesberg-Schmidt on the Danish historical culture or Menache on the Israeli one), the capture of Jerusalem in 1099 is also mentioned (e.g. Jensen on the Swedish historical culture). In the historical culture of Finland, on the contrary, the 'first' Crusade is identified as the Swedish war against Finland in 1155 (Tamminen). The perceptions of the heirs of the 'victims' or 'targets' tend to focus on the date of the first encounter with the crusaders (e.g. El-Azhari on the historical culture of Egypt), whereas many contributions did not commit to a starting date for the Crusades.

Much more pronounced are the opinions on what should be accepted as the end of the Crusades. It is not uncommon that the year 1291 is mentioned, the year that the last Roman-Christian city in the Holy Land fell: the port city of Acre (e.g. Menache on the Israeli, Chrissis on the Greek or Prietzel on the German historical culture). Furthermore, there is mention of the Third Crusade of Sweden against Finland in 1293 (cf. Tamminen), the end of the reconquista in 1492 (García-Guijarro Ramos on the Spanish, Carvalho Pinto Costa on the Portuguese historical culture) or the expulsion of the Order of Saint John from Malta (1798), which are situated temporally quite far from each other. What all of these constructions have in common is that they describe the Crusades as a phenomenon that has long since been concluded. By no means is this generally held to be true. According to our authors, in the historical cultures of Syria, Jordan and Turkey, the view that the Crusades continue to this day predominates. Ersan writes, "Today, in the Turkish public sphere the prevailing opinion is that the West never lost its interest in the Middle East. Furthermore, the obstacles the Turkish people and Turkey face in international problems – like the wars that are perpetually waged in the region – are a product of the crusader mentality".

In Arabic-speaking historical cultures, it will also matter that the Arabic term 'hurub al-faranga' ('Frankish Invasions') contains no reference to the cross, religion or 'holy war'. The Crusades are spoken of in a way that the war in Afghanistan and Iraq, as well as the deployment of Western troops (yet as per Al Zo'by, also Russian troops) in the Near East, can all be included under this term. Thus, an unbroken continuation of the phenomenon of Crusades from the Middle Ages appears (e.g. Isa on Syria).[5] With a knowledge of these interpretations, but in contrast to it, historical research in Israel (similar to the interpretation of Western Europe) focuses on the 'classical period' of the Crusades – from 1095 to 1291 (cf. Menache). Overall, it is clear that through the question of periodization, the contemporary perspectives and orientation needs are already becoming quite clear. Against this backdrop, statements such as that from the British historian Thomas Asbridge (2010) become easier to understand: "But the Crusades must also be placed where they belong: in the past".[6] At the same time, this raises the question of how historical research and historical educational offers can be conceived in a globally networked world if a position that is much divided in Western Europe, such as that of Asbridge, is not at all capable of consensus in international comparison.

In order to gain an overview of the diversity of the dates and facts considered important, the most prominent of them have been compiled. Table 4.1 provides a register of concrete references to the past that are mentioned in the contributions. Those mentioned by more than one contributor are listed in bold. The essentially well-known dates are complimented by a selection of dates only mentioned once in order to clarify the temporal, geographical and content range of interpretations.

On the one hand, the years printed in bold show that there are certainly some dates that are repeatedly mentioned. On the other hand, from 27 contributions, only 16 dates are mentioned by more than one contributor; and from these, three do not refer to the same event and four of them are only mentioned by two contributors. This results in only 12 events (from which hardly any source material can be cited for the Children's Crusade) that were considered to be relevant to the history of the Crusades by three or more contributors. The leading dates were 1099 (seven), 1095 (six), 1096 (three or four) as well as 1291 (six). Opposite these are 50 dates, of which not all were listed here, that were only mentioned in *one single* contribution.[7] Scarcely could a different quantitative analysis better illustrate just how disparate the phenomenon of the Crusades is understood.

For a qualitative interpretation, it is worth looking at some historical myths that were cited, such as the previously mentioned 'Children's Crusade' (in the Belgian and Netherlands historical cultures, cf. Hemptienne and van Moolenbroek). Within the political–historical understanding, 'myth' means an empirically invalid narrative that is, nevertheless, held to be true, or formerly held to be true – i.e. a historical half-truth or a legend. They can form out of a lack of knowledge or intentionally. Myths can be dealt with collectively, as poly-myths, or as autocratically initiated and even controlled, as mono-myths. Regarding the functions of the myth – which can take on any conceivable narrative form – is the foundation of identity by means of emotional mobilization and the collective rallying behind a particular goal. In this light, it is obvious that the Crusades provide the material from which myths are born – especially in the form of poly-myths.[8] In the

Table 4.2 Myths of the Crusades mentioned in the articles

Alleged date	*Myth*	*Author*	*Country*
1155	Lalli, the Finn, slays Bishop Henry of Uppsala during the First Swedish Crusade in Finland.	Tamminen	Finland
1190	'A myth created around 1400 in Haarlem, the second city of the county of Holland. Here, the conquest of Damietta was linked to the Third Crusade and the Emperor Frederick I Barbarossa. According to this story, the emperor could only conquer the chain-protected harbour of Damietta thanks to an action of crusaders from Haarlem along with young William of Holland, the future Count. They attached toothed iron to the bow and keel of a sailing ship, and sailed the harbour chain in pieces, allowing the city to be captured. As a reward, the Haarlem crusaders received a new coat of arms for their city from the hands of the emperor and the patriarch of Jerusalem'.	van Moolenbroek	Netherlands
1219	'According to legend, the flag – a much used symbol of Danish identity which carries great value for many Danes – fell from the sky during a battle in Estonia. The story appeared in the early 16th-century writings of two Danish historians, Christiern Pedersen and Peder Olesen, who drew on material now lost. They ascribed the event to a battle in 1208, but from the late 16th century it became associated with the Battle of Lyndanisse (Estonia), which took place on 15 June 1219'.	Fonnesberg-Schmidt	Denmark
1920	'"Wake up Saladin, we are back again!" proclaimed Henri Gouraud as he kicked the grave of Saladin in Damascus in 1920'.	Isa	Syria

contribution on Belgium, Hemptinne even cites the oeuvre of Anne Morelli (ed.) as an important literature, *Les grands mythes de l'histoire de Belgique, de Flandre et de Wallonie* [The great Myths of the History of Belgium, Flanders and Wallonia], Brussels, 1995.

The four myths mentioned in Table 4.2 can be interpreted as founding myths. Lalli is this in the sense that he is the 'First Finn' as he makes a stand against Swedish dominance. William I of the Netherlands is to be ennobled as the founder of the Netherlands due to his 'heroic deed' in concert of powers of the emperor led Crusade. However, the Third Crusade by no means conquered Damietta – and certainly not under Barbarossa. The legend of the heavenly flag, of Denmark, which does not even receive an attempt of rational explanation, but for the author, serves as a foundation myth. (The national symbol of Denmark is not up for debate *because* the flag fell from the sky.) The relation to the final myth mentioned in the table concerns the mythical, embellished story of the betrayal of the victorious European countries of the First World War to the Arabs.

Overall, the comparison of all the concrete references to the past mentioned in the texts shows how dependant they are on perspectives and of orientation. This also applies to the historical myths that fulfil the societal function of temporal orientation, although they cannot be empirically proven (at least at a certain core). This leads directly to a reflection on the dimensions of historical culture.

4. To what extent can the descriptions of historical cultures be more precisely characterized in the different dimensions?

As presented in Ch. 2, historical cultures can be described in five dimensions. Jörn Rüsen differentiates between the *cognitive*, *aesthetic*, *political*, *moral* and *religious* dimensions. These dimensions will be treated sequentially, beginning with the cognitive dimension, wherein historiography is the initial focus.

To what extent do the contributors speak about historiography? For one thing, within the contributions, it is frequently mentioned that national histories have been strongly internationalized in recent decades. In the texts presented in this volume, Jensen (the author of the contribution on Sweden) is also quoted by Fonnesberg-Schmidt for Denmark. And the misjudged Carl Erdmann (*The Origin of the Idea of Crusade*, 1935) is not only mentioned by Prietzel on Germany, but also by Kostick on Ireland. Moreover, one can assume that foundational works are quite well known, such as *A history of the Crusades* by Steven Runciman (1950–1954).

The prevalence of these works is certainly closely linked to linguistic knowledge and the availability of translations. It is noteworthy that, of all things, the formerly most important historiography of France is hardly mentioned internationally. Herein emerges a significant research potential of an international, comparative history of historiography.

Then again, historically contingent focuses in the respective historiographies become apparent. The contrasts within the historiography of the history of the Crusades, as differentiated earlier, are an expression of the differences of historical cultures, and demonstrate just how historiography as an institution is embedded in historical cultures. For instance, this becomes clear upon comparing the coverage of the Polish and Georgian historians, both being strongly influenced by national perspectives. The differences are remarkable. While Tsurtsumia emphasizes the historiography of Georgia in the Soviet era – how much the Crusades of Marxist historiography followed a materialistic interpretation – this does not appear in Polejowski's summary of the historiography of Poland. In fact, historiography is partly conceived as an antagonism for the non-academic historical culture. An outright contrast to this is noted for the Netherlands by van Moolenbroek, for Israel by Menache and for Jordan by Al Zo'by. They emphasize historiography as an authority that operates as a moderating corrective against the political and religious abuse of the history of the Crusades through politics and the public sphere. From this, the following thesis can be derived: on the whole, the ambivalence of historiography in the context of a historical culture becomes clear; it oscillates between the poles of societal and political acceptance and critical distance.

The aesthetical dimension of historical cultures is especially noticeable in films and historical novels. The underlying thesis is that a story must be told 'well', that is, aesthetical criteria must be satisfied in order for it to be acknowledged by society. If one were to go through the contributions, it would be noticeable that novels are especially mentioned, in particular Walter Scott, *The Talisman* 1825 (Horswell & Phillips on Great Britain) and Thea Beckman, *Kruistocht in spijkerbroek*/*Crusade in Jeans* 1973 (Hemtinne on Belgium, van Moolenbroek on the Netherlands). Further examples include the Estonian novel, *Ümera jõel* [*At the Ümera river*] (1934) by Mait Metsanurk (Selart), Μαρία Δοξαπατρή [*Maria Doxapatri*] by Dimitrios Bernardakis (1858) by Chrissis, the Georgian novel by Konstantine Gamsakhurdia, *Davit aghmashenebeli* [*David the Builder*] from 1946 to 1958 (Tsurtsumia) or Amos Oz's short story, *Unto Death* from 1971 (Menache). Torquato Tasso's epic, *Gerusalemme liberata* [*Jerusalem Delivered*] (1581), is credited by Russo as still having a rather powerful influence in Italy. Additionally, some films are also mentioned in the articles, for example, the Swedish film *Arn – Tempelriddaren* (2007) (Jensen), which goes back to a cycle of novels of the Swedish author Jan Guillou, or the film *Crusade in Jeans* (Ben Sombogaard, 2006) (Hemptinne on Belgium).

At times, historical culture is also cited in the context of sports. According to Tsurtsumia, the "nickname of the Georgian national teams in football and basketball is the *Crusaders*". Another example can be found in England, where there are Rugby teams called *Saracens* and *Crusaders* (Horswell & Phillips). Additionally, Polejowski mentions an active historical reenactment in Poland on the occasion of the anniversary of the 1410 Grunwald/Tannenberg battle against the Teutonic Order.

This picture appears diverse; yet, it cannot be generalized. Concerning the Turkish historical culture, Ersan writes that despite the general acceptance of the political reality of the phenomenon of Crusades,

> there is no noteworthy reflection of this in the Turkish film industry, culture, or literature. There has not been a film produced or a book written that has impressed the masses, nor has a museum of the Crusades been founded.

Sometimes, the authors do not go into details about historical novels, films, etc.; this does not automatically mean that corresponding literature and films are not there. A more specific exploration of the aesthetic dimension of historical cultures in an international comparison would be extraordinarily exciting, one that would better identify which historical details (persons, objects, structures, events) are aestheticized, as well as why and by what means – for example, to what degree do they refer to historical artist creations from or around the time of the Crusades.

The political dimension of historical cultures resonates within all the contributions, and given its importance for the historical construct of meaning, it cannot be otherwise. Already with the Crusades of the Middle Ages, but not limited to them, it was about dominance in the Near East and Middle East, as well as the Baltics and the Iberian Peninsula. Until this day, the Middle Eastern region is a centre of conflict of global importance. Of note is the connection made to the Crusades by the US President George W. Bush following the 2001 terrorist attacks. As described by Pegg, his politics were explicitly placed in this tradition. This example is also clearly present in the contribution of Syria. Isa explicitly speaks of the feeling many Syrians have of a "state of continuous rape and violation" by the West.

The political dimension is even more definitive in the contribution by Bagdasarjan on the historical culture of Russia. Much of his text is about the USA, although America could have in no way been a part of the Crusades of the Middle Ages. An interpretation emerges here that does not refer to the Crusades of the Middle Ages, showing just how flexible this metaphor can be applied within different political contexts. The following can be concluded: particularly in every interpretation wherein the affirmative-factual-traditional construct of meaning dominates, the political dimension plays a large role, as the Crusades are viewed as a continuous phenomenon. Furthermore, the political dimension is clearly present in the contributions when political breaks are mentioned – i.e. the end of the Second World War (Prietzel on Germany), the terrorist attacks of 9/11 (e.g. Pegg on the USA) or the dissolution of the Eastern Block (e.g. Selart on Estonia – as well as Fonnesberg-Schmidt on Denmark). In all cases mentioned, the authors give an account of a reorientation, and partly of a revaluation of the phenomenon of the 'Crusades' in light of a new political situation. To take up the latter example, according to Selart, in Estonia, the idea of a threat from Germany prevailed until 1990, imagined as Teutonic Knights no less. However, after 1990, the majority of Estonians aspired to emancipate themselves from Russia. Within this context, they saw the history of the Crusades, and also Germany, in a more open, nuanced and international way. Apprehending these political developments, Denmark re-established contact with Estonia, its former county, and suddenly began to become interested in its own role in the history of the Baltic Crusades (Fonnesberg-Schmidt).

In the contributions collected here, there is clearly a political importance, either former or even current, placed on the monuments in remembrance of the Crusades. The monuments listed in Table 4.3 are mentioned in the texts:

There are other monuments, and perhaps some that were formerly more important, such as Saladin's in Damascus (Abdallah al-Sayed, 1933) or the German 'Tannenberg Memorial' (Walter and Johannes Krüger, 1935). Yet, it is certainly significant that they were *not* mentioned by our authors. Evidently, the political auspices have changed, resulting in their loss of importance.

Also, there are times that the authors comment very explicitly on the moral dimension. In accordance with how they are commonly presented today, the Crusades stuck with being assessed as unjust, if not reprehensible. This is particularly clear in Isa's contribution on Syria, but applies to the dominant interpretations in Estonia and Poland. Contrarily, in Georgia, the interpretation that the Crusades should be

Table 4.3 Monuments related to the Crusades mentioned in the articles

Date	*Figure or event*	*Location*	*Sculptor, architect*	*Author*
1848	Godfrey of Bouillon	Belgium: Royal Square at Brussels	Eugène Simonis	Hemptinne
1860	Richard I of England, "the Lionheart"	Great Britain: In front of House of Commons, London	Carlo Marochetti	Hoswell & Phillips
1868	Baldwin I, Latin Emperor	Belgium: Mons	Joseph Jaquet	Hemptinne
1874	Peter the Hermit	France: Amiens	Gédéon de Forceville	Hemptinne
1989	Lalli ("the first of all Fins")	Finland: Satakunta	Aimo Tukiainen	Tamminen
2012	Jean de Valette	Malta: Pjazza Jean de Vallette, Valletta	Joseph Chetcuti	Buttigieg

evaluated in a positive light dominates, because the Crusades led to the liberation from the Suljuks (Tsurtsumia). Substantial differences are revealed here.

A salient instance is the reception of Sultan Saladin (Salah ad-Din), who reconquered Jerusalem from the Crusaders in 1189.[9] The values that he is supposed to embody are by no means consistent. It happens that Al Azhari reports that in Egypt Saladin serves as the central figure of Islamic terrorism no less. Entirely the other way around, Aavitsland points out that a 'Saladin-Day' was introduced in Norway in 2009 and is "an annual festival dedicated to political and religious dialogue, literature, debates, and lectures, often with a focus on Middle East culture". These two interpretations could not be further from each other.

We finally arrive at the religious dimension of historical culture. It will become clear that the religious dimension carries more importance in some historical cultures than others. "In present day Swedish society", according to Jensen, "The Crusades are generally seen as a deplorable misunderstanding of Christianity". Moreover, he states that, "Historians in Sweden have not begun to explain the medieval Crusades as the necessary defence against the inherent violent religion of Islam, as has happened internationally in some cases since 2001". Additionally, religious motives are dealt with in more detail in the contributions by Pegg (USA) and Bagdasarjan (Russia).

It is abundantly clear how extensively the religious and political dimensions of historical cultures condition each other and even mix together. Pegg explains how, within the historical culture of the USA, under President George W. Bush, the 'War on Terror' was designated as a 'Crusade' in 2001. During 2016, the then presidential candidate Donald Trump avoided this connection, moving the theme of the 'clash of civilisations' (Huntington) to the forefront. In comparison, the Crusades are increasingly popular in the prevalent interpretations within Islamic fundamentalist perspectives. Contrarily in Bagdasarjan's contribution on Russia, he laments the loss of the importance of religion. In perceived secular attitude of the West, he tends to see a threat. Al-Zo'by, when writing on the non-academic historical culture of Jordan, notes that the Crusades signify a "cosmic struggle between Islam and Christianity", while military, geographical or economical interpretive patterns predominate in Jordanian historiography.

In contrast to this, Bagdasarjan stresses that within the Russian historical culture, the interpretation predominates that Russia is the strongest bulwark against US-American, and Western in general, crusading ambitions.

Remarkably, Bagdasarjan does not see the problem in the militant-Christian zeal of the USA, but the reverse, in the secularization of the West. He perceives secularization, which is now expansively pursued, as the threat to Russian identity, the core of this identity being Russian Orthodoxy and the peaceful cohabitation with other religions.

That the Crusades are not interpreted in the religious dimension within historiography, while they are in non-academic historical culture, such interpretative patterns prominently appear. This shows a commonality within historiography. The historians cited in Ch. 3 employ a secular means of interpretation, that is, they explicate history as something made by humans (while the chroniclers of the Middle Ages described the crusaders as an instrument of God). This counts – despite all the differences in interpretation – as one of the commonalities among the self-perception of contemporary cultures of historiography, which is clear in the texts presented here. At the same time, a great potential for conflict is revealed in that drastically different political and military actives are justified by the history of the Crusades in historical cultures, and references to religious patterns of interpretation are made.

5. Concluding remarks

This comparison of the reception of the Crusades, which is by no means exhaustive, shows just how multifaceted and controversial this history is within historical cultures. This shows both the functions and interpretative patterns that are dominant in each case. One commonality is that among all the historical cultures presented here, the concept, or the equivalent, of 'Crusade' exists, while the interpretations concerning it are massively different. It can be assumed that what are being dealt with here are societal conventions of historical thinking which only become discernible in comparison.

As demonstrated earlier, this use of historical conventions becomes very plastic within the narratives on the Crusades. This phenomenon appears in additional historiography. For example, only in British historiography are the activities of Edward I spoken of as an independent Crusade. The fact that the present work is not to depict small subtleties, but to express contemporary perspectives of historians on the Crusades should become clear through a comparison of the earlier texts.

While this book is in development, there is a war in Syria. Even if none of the authors mention this, it is obvious that even for the most diverse actors the history of the Crusades is a relevant (political) subject. In this context, one might speculate that the West – not least due to the demonstrable power of mobilization under an always latent charge that the West 'would yet again lead a Crusade' – has operated especially restrained in Syria only daring to use covert ground forces. The historiography of the Crusades should be seen within the context of historical cultures, and exists within political, moral, aesthetic and religious patterns of interpretation that are relevant for society.

Notes

1 Udo Kuckartz, *Qualitative Text Analysis. Methods, Practice, Computer Assistance* (London, 2014).

2 Since the focus is on the product of historical thinking, and not the process of it, the methods cannot be questioned; yet, the decisions relating to the selection and definition of persons and events that were made on the basis of the methods can be questioned.

3 Charlotte Gauthier and Jonathan Phillips (eds.), *The Crusades and the Far-Right in the 21st Century* (Engaging the Crusades, volumes 8+9) (London/New York, forthcoming).

4 There is a large amount of agreement within academic literature regarding the number of Oriental Crusades up to and including the Fourth Crusade, which culminated in the conquering of Constantinople by the Latins in 1204. However, after the Fourth Crusade, differing emphases start to predominate. For instance, in German academic research, there are a total of seven Crusades, in English academic research nine, whereas in French eight. This is not explicitly a subject in the texts presented here, yet it is a significant backdrop for the one who wishes to understand them (cf. the

Wikipedia-article 'Kreuzzug' https://de.wikipedia.org/wiki/Kreuzzug, 'Crusades' https://en.wikipedia.org/wiki/Crusades and 'Croisades' https://fr.wikipedia.org/wiki/Croisades (all were accessed 26.04.2019).

5 It can also be pointed out that the divisions of historical eras – Antiquity, the Middle Ages, Modern Times – were made in and for Europe. In cultures outside of Europe – also the Arabic cultures – these categories can be conditionally employed, if necessary. If the break between the eras of the Middle Ages and the modern is removed, it is easier to suggest interpreting and accepting the continuation of phenomena that are considered 'typically medieval' from a European perspective. This subject was not explicitly taken up in the short contributions, yet was apparently often subtlely assumed (Editor's note).

6 Thomas Asbridge, The Crusades. The War for the Holy Land (London, 2010), p. 681.

7 The publication dates of written works, such as periods and ranges of time, were not taken into account (which would have gone considerably too far).

8 Nikolas Jaspert, 'Ein Polymythos: Die Kreuzzüge' (A Polymyth: The Crusades), in *Mythen der Geschichte (Myths of History)*, eds. Helmut Altrichter, Klaus Herbes, Helmut Neuhaus (Freiburg, 2004), pp. 203–235.

9 Indeed, paradoxically, apart from the Shia, today the entire world sees Saladin as a moral role model. While the native-born Kurd is often simply received as an idol of militant Arabic resistance, he belongs to the tradition of Gotthold Ephraim Lessing (*Nathan the Wise*, 1779), as an Enlightenment example of humanity, wisdom, leniency and all kinds of chivalrous virtues of a ruler.

5 Historical education under the conditions of conflicting narratives in a globalized world

Felix Hinz and Johannes Meyer-Hamme

A comparison of the contributions convincingly shows just how differently the history of the Crusades is conceived. Essentially, the contributions point out that today the Crusades are not only to be dealt with as a phenomenon of the Middle Ages, but also that their reception considered, as well as how they are negotiated within historical cultures. It turns out that in the different historical cultures, the context of meaning between "perceptions of the past, present understanding and future perspectives"[1] is construed quite differently. From this grows the perception that when dealing with history, one must always pass between the poles of 'us today' and 'the others today', as well as 'us back then' and 'the others back then'. Yet, the internal divisions and the high amount of diversity within the postulated groups must always be taken into account. And this has repercussions for historical education. In an increasingly inter-connected world – not least in it being characterized by large migration – people refer to entirely different narrations and, therefore, to differing identities and orientation offerings. Today, every individual must continually react to different narratives about the past which can drastically change over the course of time, revealed by a number of the aforementioned contributions. Thus, it must be considered that within the perspective of didactics of history, the Crusades of the Middle Ages cannot be the sole focus, as it would not be clear to what extent present-day constructs are being applied. Neither should only contemporary perspectives be considered, like how the past is spoken of in the historical cultures. While the first option would be ahistorical, as the question of contemporary orientations needs would not be taken into account. The second option would be purely sociological. It is much more a question of how relations of meaning can be drawn among different events from the past and how implications can be drawn for the future. This leads to the question of how historical learning can be formulated if historians cannot agree on common narratives and suggest different conclusions for the present and future.

> What are history teachers to do with the ubiquitous discrepancy, conflict and contradiction among historical interpretations that are the lifeblood of academic history? After we acknowledge that there is not one, true history that "matches" the past, how can the morass of relativism be avoided? What guidance is available?[2]

This question was formulated by Peter Seixas in 2016 at a symposium on history didactics. Foundational to didactical considerations of this kind are the ontological differences between past (as necessary passing) and history as retrospective narration on the past. It is requisite of these narratives that they have both a perspective and are selective. In this respect, the outcome of the present volume is not an exception, but rather the normal case. The fact that people come into contact with different narratives in the course of their lives is also involved. They come into contact with various narratives and adopt a perspective about them and, from this backdrop, develop their historical consciousness. Hence, the question arises: how historical learning can be conceived under the conditions of a globally inter-connected world, wherein people come into contact and must communicate and deal with others who have an entirely differently formed historical consciousness. In the year 2000, this question was posed by Peter Seixas in the backdrop of postmodern historical theory. He discussed three possible answers:

- Teaching 'the best history of the past' according to a master narrative formulated through the consensus of experts of history (this is often within a national context). In its socio-historical dimension, historical learning seeks to produce 'collective memories', which are to be endowed with identity, cohesion and a common moral framework. A critical objection is that such claims are aimed at homogenous societies and reinforce the differences and conflicts in historical orientation among societies. Furthermore, learning about history for students becomes nothing more than reproducing prepared interpretations, which are not uncommonly seen as a collection of meaningless names and events.
- Teaching 'history as a way of knowing' seeks to bring the principles of historical learning into focus, and that those learning develop the ability to deal with their own historical questions. This approach "should help them to develop the ability and the

disposition to arrive independently at reasonable, informed opinions".[3] One aspect of this concept can be criticized insofar as it stands in opposition to the goal, stated earlier, of the production of collective memories. At the same time, it hides the radical nature of the open questions of historiography from those learning.

- Teaching uncertainty is the postmodern position. What is meant is "that all knowledge is an expression of position and power, to believe Hayden White's argument that historians impose narratives on the inchoate past as a literary trick akin to the work of novelists".[4] If the postmodern theoretician is to be endorsed, then this position should not be withheld from students – Seixas ironically plays with this notion in the title of his article. However, it was critically noted that 'anything' goes might become possible. Yet, it brings up the question as to why history should even be taught.[5]

These three answers can also be applied to the history of the Crusades. Advocates of the first approach formulate a 'master narrative' of the Crusades and seek to make it mandatory for history lessons. School books frequently offer a clear-cut interpretation of the Crusades and do not make the controversy surrounding them a subject. Advocates of the second approach allow differing narratives to be compared and work with students to determine the degree to which they differ. This type of teaching aims to, taking the example of the history of the Crusades, bring the 'grammar of historical thinking' into focus.[6] The advocates of the third approach, which is far less differentiated, would de-construct the dominant narratives within a society as expressions of perspective and power.

The conception of didactical conclusions refers to foundational historical, theoretical and societal aspects. The area of tension of historical educational concepts stretches between the poles of history lessons being endowed by collective memories or of the complete support of individual appropriation when dealing with history.

In the following, a cursory look will be given to the most influential didactic models of historical thinking and learning, in order to be able to discuss the question of the didactical consequences of the findings on the history of the Crusades presented earlier.

All of the great models of didactics of history, which were developed in academic scholarship (in pluralistic countries), are constructed upon the position that history is a construct of the past based on a perspective. Furthermore, we live in an inter-connected world, wherein people must communicate with each other, people who were socialized in entirely different historical cultures and who justifiably trust different historical narratives. This conjecture is once again substantiated in the texts on historical cultures on the history of the Crusades. Additionally, since it remains unclear which historical orientation is persuasive for those learning, or what they advocate for outside of school,[7] which historical orientations will be relevant for the future lives of those learning cannot be estimated. The aim of the following approaches mentioned is discerning transferable concepts and abilities. Therefore, historical instruction in school is aimed at enabling young people to have independent and critically reflective contact with the past and history.

We are aware that within the West, as well as outside it, opinion exists that the inter-connected world is more of a threat than a chance. This stance encourages strengthening borders and to keeping nations 'pure'. The first of the possible answers formulated by Peter Seixas follows such political considerations. However, in what follows, we prefer to turn to those history didactic models which were formulated by the other answers regarding the diversity of the narratives. Early on, Peter Lee and Rosalyn Ashby grappled with the question of how learners explain the differences between contradictory historical narrations.[8] The foundation insight is that students are confronted with contradictory narratives in their environment – and all the more today in the age of social media! Therefore, they suggest that the central goals of historical learning lie in concepts that are transmitted historically. They designated these as second-order concepts. A conception of history itself is contained in such concepts. The concepts vary between very naïve and very elaborate forms among adolescents. In Lee and Ashby's famous study, they presented two contradictory narratives on the history of the Roman Empire. In one of the narratives, the Roman Empire fell in 476 CE and in the other it fell in 1453 CE. They then had the subjects of the study explain how historians could come to such different assertions. The answers varied between the idea that only one narrative could be correct, and the idea that the narratives were formed by differing perspectives which brought about the differences. Some of the subjects recognized that in the example provided, it depended on the question of whether the 'Eastern Empire' was accepted as the 'Roman Empire', or if the concept only referred to the 'Western Empire'.

Peter Seixas pursues a very similar approach. His approach demonstrated that adolescents in Canada only very partially perceived the content of their history classes to be relevant to their own lives. Of far greater importance were the stories that they had learned in their own environment (especially in their family and peer group).[9] This is also due to the fact that it is not the responsibility of the history instructor to provide an answer as to which stories are relevant for particular individuals. Employing this logic, history courses should help to develop elaborate concepts on the subject, which Seixas likewise designates as second-order concepts. From this basis, he argues that second-order concepts should be made a subject of historical learning.[10] He suggests some which should be valid for anyone working with history. His insights include the following:

- establish historical significance
- use primary source evidence
- identify continuity and change
- analyse cause and consequence
- take historical perspectives, and understand the ethical dimension of historical interpretations.[11]

These second-order concepts can also be applied to an analysis of the history of the Crusades. Academic scholarship, the state and teachers cannot decide which interpretation out of the many competing interpretations of the Crusades that exist is solely the right one. However, they can differentiate between statements which are supported by sources and those which are contradictory. Because of this, didactics aim to provide students with concepts so that they can (as they must) decide which, and why, some historical constructs of meaning are persuasive for them. The didactic idea behind this is to make these applicable insights the central theme in selected examples. This approach belongs to the second answer of the postmodern challenge.

Sam Wineburg represents another approach.[12] He suggests, not least due to changes in social media, a more precise examination of documents in order to decide to what degree the information is plausible. In a first step, a document is to be considered as a source and questioned regarding when and by whom it was written, for what purpose and its credibility. Wineburg calls this step ‘sourcing’. In the second step, the students are to contextualize the source within its historical situation (‘contextualization’), in order to proceed to the third step, where the document is read more closely and commented on (‘close reading’). In the fourth step, it is a matter of classification, drawing on contextual knowledge of the document and information provided in order to proceed to the final step. The final step consists of searching for other sources that either support or contradict the information (‘corroboration’). Similar to the second-order concepts, Wineburg pursues the goal of gaining transferable knowledge by historical learning. Admittedly, the focus for Wineburg is on general critical thinking skills and not particularly on critically dealing with the past and history. He does differentiate between the levels of novices and experts. They are differentiated insofar as novices hardly scrutinize source material, while the experts, before delivering an assessment of the credibility of the source, ask about the author, time period, the literary genre, etc.[13] With such a perspective, the different approaches to the Crusades could be questioned by the strategy described earlier in order to decide whether the interpretations offered can be considered credible or not. Consequently, Wineburg's concept should also be assigned to the second answer of historical learning of postmodernism, despite its large differences with the second-order concepts approach.

Clearly, more comprehensive is the competence model of historical thinking of the international group, including Waltraud Schreiber, Andreas Körber, among others.[14] It is based on the narrative theoretical thoughts of Arthur Danto[15] and Jörn Rüsen,[16] in that history is understood as 'constructions of meaning'. Dealing with orientation in time in the form of historical narrations is thereby moved to the centre of reflection. Historical thinking is described as being able to comprehensively deal with the past and history.

The competence model of historical thinking goes beyond the considerations thus far in three aspects. First, this model differentiates between procedural competencies and a categorical competence. On this basis, the thoughts regarding second-order concepts[17] as well as historical thinking skills are combined. Historical subject matter competencies are described as having command over categories and concepts. Historical thinking skills are differentiated between competencies in inquiring historically, competencies in applying historical methods and competencies in historical orientation in time. Thus, the narrative logic of the temporal orientation of historical thinking is differentiated into three fields of competencies. In this sense, historical competencies are more than merely skills that can be mechanically applied. Instead, as pointedly formulated, they are "domain specific problem-solving skills that produce creative solutions".[18] In other words, they are skills, techniques, rules and particular abilities that can be continually applied to new situations and subject matter. Someone who masters the rules of chess is by no means a good chess player. In order to be one, it is essential to continually devise new and creative strategies to achieve the goal.

Second, these historical competencies are not only to be applied so that the creation of one's own historical narrations is the focus, but also to deal critically with the historical narratives of others. In this respect, the re-construction of the past in the form of historical narratives and the de-construction of historical narratives are differentiated. This difference is all the more relevant as most people do not narrate history themselves, but must deal with completed historical narratives presented in the media every day. If the theory is correct, that those in a globalized inter-connected world people with different narrations regarding the history of the Crusades come into contact with each other, and have to work with each other, then a deconstruction of these narratives is required. And a history lesson can serve as a great place for this to be learned.

The third particularity of this model is that it not only differentiates areas of historical thinking, but levels as well. The extent to which historical thinking can draw upon societal conventions will be shown. In the texts on the Crusades in the different historical cultures, completely differing interpretations, which are recognized socially, are presented.[19] Especially in a comparison, it is clear that it is a matter of conventions of historical thinking. Such conventions are necessary to be able to communicate. At the same time, it is about contemporary conventions of the past. The competence model of historical thinking makes a distinction regarding the extent to which such conventions can be drawn upon. If someone possesses one of these conventions, and can employ it, then she or he possesses a middle competence level, designated as having a conventional level. If someone does not know such conventions, but rather has to respond spontaneously and situationally, she or he possesses a basic competence level, which is designated as having an a-conventional level. If someone knows these conventions and reflects on them as conventions and constructions, then the competence level is designated as elaborate, or trans-conventional.[20] Taking the example of the history of the Crusades, it can be pointed out that the narratives or the direction of view regarding the Crusades can be taken as conventional interpretations. Whoever has such interpretations and is able to communicate that in society has a middle level, provided that she or he does not know about reflecting on the logic of constructions. Whoever does not have such interpretations, dealing with such interpretations spontaneously and situationally, has a base level.

On the basis of these considerations, the different conventions of historical narration on the history of the Crusades will be compared and questioned. This includes which interests and functions they serve, on which sources they are based, which interpretive patterns are applied and, finally, what historical orientation do they provide. In this sense, historical learning is a means of acquiring foundational forms and concepts of historical thinking by the de-construction of historical narratives in order to apply these independently later in life. Here is also an approach that is close to the second possible answer to historical learning in postmodernity as presented by Peter Seixas. These concepts can be thought about from the background of the present publication. In view of the significantly different conceptions of the history of the Crusades – as is abundantly clear in the texts presented – in an international comparison, de-constructing these historical narratives is hardly enough. This is indeed a necessary step, but in no way it is sufficiently dealing with the matter. Johannes Meyer-Hamme has differentiated three dimensions of historical learning:[21]

1 If the goal of historical learning is focusing on transferable skills and concepts of historical thinking, then the focus of historical learning should be the independent historical narration (re-construction), as well as dealing with the historical narrations of others (de-construction). At the same time, the concepts and categories of historical thinking must be discussed in a similar fashion as the concept of history, made clear in the study by Peter Lee and Rosalyn Ashby. In this respect, historical learning can be described as an elaboration of the competencies of historical thinking, similar to how it is described in the competence model of historical thinking.
2 If every instance of historical learning is situated in a historical culture, then historical learning is, at the same time, an introduction to the respective historical culture. Therefore, the perspectives, interpretations as well as concepts that are employed are those which are compatible in society. On the history of the Crusades, some authors referred to textbooks. In comparison, it becomes quite clear how they can be understood as mediums of historical cultures. They can also be designated as 'national autobiographies'.[22] Yet if historical learning is also an introduction to historical cultures, each respective historical culture, within a globally inter-connected world, should itself be an object of reflection. Why history is told in the way that is within society should be a point of inquiry. A comparison of different approaches is well suited for this task.
3 When there are entirely differing approaches to a historical subject, such as the history of the Crusades, and at the same time there being no way to reach a scholarly decision regarding which approach is correct, then learners should be at liberty to position themselves within the social discourse. This leads to the question

> of which histories can be recognized and which ones cannot. A distinction must be made between the many historical narratives that can exist alongside each other, and those which are not supported by historical sources, or even contradict source material. While the former can legitimately exist side by side in history classes, the narratives that can be refuted empirically should be indicated as such and their validity judged accordingly.[23]

This concept of historical learning goes beyond the second possible answer of historical learning in postmodernity by Peter Seixas, not only in its focus on the principles and concepts of historical thinking, but also insofar as the concrete interpretations of the past – as they are formulated in society – are a point of focus. Additionally, this concept inquires as to which perspectives and interpretations of society prevail and are recognized, and which are not. To what extent this pertains how history is dealt with will become abundantly clear in the following material.

Notes

1 Karl-Ernst Jeismann, 'Geschichtsbewusstsein' (Historical Consciousness), in *Handbuch der Geschichtsdidaktik (Handbook for Didactics of History)*, ed. Klaus Bergmann e.a. (Düsseldorf, 1985), pp. 42–44.
2 Peter Seixas, 'Narrative Interpretation in History (and Life)', in *Begriffene Geschichte – Geschichte Begreifen (History Grasped – Grasp History). Essays in Honour of Jörn Rüsen*, ed. Holger Thünemann (Frankfurt a.M., 2016), pp. 83–99, here: p. 99.
3 Peter Seixas, 'Schweigen! Die Kinder! or Does Postmodern History Have a Place in the Schools?', in *Knowing, Teaching and Learning History. National and International Perspectives*, ed. Peter Seixas et al. (New York, 2000), pp. 19–37, here: pp. 24–25.
4 Peter Seixas, 'Narrative Interpretation in History (and Life)', in *Begriffene Geschichte*, pp. 83–99, here: p. 83.
5 Peter Seixas, 'Schweigen!', pp. 19–37.
6 Bodo von Borries, *Historisch Denken Lernen – Welterschließung statt Epochenüberblick. Geschichte als Unterrichtsfach und Bildungsaufgabe (Learning to Think Historically – Opening up the World Instead of Looking at Epochs. History as a Teaching Subject and Educational Task)* (Opladen and Farmington Hills, 2008).
7 Peter Seixas, 'Historical Understanding Among Adolescents in a Multicultural Setting', *Curriculum Inquiry* 23, 3 (1993), pp. 301–327; Johannes Meyer-Hamme, *Historische Identitäten und Geschichtsunterricht. Fallstudien zum Verhältnis von kultureller Zugehörigkeit, schulischen Anforderungen und individueller Verarbeitung (Historical Identities and History Education: Case Studies on the Relationship between Cultural Affiliation, School Requirements and Individual Processing)* (Idstein, 2009).

8 Peter Lee, R. Ashby, 'Progression in Historical Understanding among Students Age 7–14', in *Knowing, Teaching, and Learning History. National and International Perspectives*, eds. Peter N. Stearns, Peter Seixas, Sam Wineburg (New York, 2000), pp. 199–222.
9 Peter Seixas, 'Historical Understanding', pp. 301–327.
10 Peter Seixas, Tom Morton, *The Big Six Historical Thinking Concepts* (Toronto, 2012).
11 Ibid.
12 Samuel S. Wineburg, Daisy Martin, Chauncey Monte-Sano, *Reading like a Historian: Teaching Literacy in Middle and High School History Classrooms* (New York, 2013).
13 Peter Seixas, Tom Morton, *The Big Six*.
14 Andreas Körber, Waltraud Schreiber, Alexander Schöner (eds.), *Kompetenzen historischen Denkens. Ein Strukturmodell als Beitrag zur Kompetenzorientierung in der Geschichtsdidaktik (Competences of Historical Thinking. A Structural Model as a Contribution to Competence Orientation in History Didactics)* (Neuried, 2007); Andreas Körber, 'Historical Thinking and Historical Competencies as Didactic Core Concepts', in *Teaching Historical Memories in an Intercultural Perspective. Concepts and Methods. Experiences and Results from the TeacMem Project*, eds. Helle Bjerg, Andreas Körber, Claudia Lenz, Oliver von Wrochem (Berlin, 2014), pp. 69–96.
15 Arthur C. Danto, *Analytical Philosophy of History* (Cambridge, 1965).
16 Jörn Rüsen, *Evidence and Meaning: A Theory of Historical Studies* (New York, 2017).
17 Peter Lee, R. Ashby, 'Progression in Historical Understanding', pp. 199–222); Peter Seixas, Tom Morton, *The Big Six*.
18 Hans-Jürgen Pandel, *Geschichtsdidaktik. Eine Theorie für die Praxis (History Didactics. A Theory for Practice)* (Schwalbach/Ts., 2013), p. 208.
19 For questions regarding dating, see Chapter 4.
20 Andreas Körber, 'Niveaus der Verfügung über einen Quellenbegriff. Eine Skizze der Graduierung einer Einzelkompetenz im Bereich der historischen Sachkompetenz(en)' (Levels of Disposal of a Source Concept. A Sketch of the Graduation of an Individual Competence in the Field of Historical Subject Competence(s)), in Andreas Körber et al., *Kompetenzen*, pp. 546–562.
21 Johannes Meyer-Hamme, 'Was heißt historisches Lernen? Eine Begriffsbestimmung im Spannungsfeld gesellschaftlicher Anforderungen, subjektiver Bedeutungszuschreibungen und Kompetenzen historischen Denkens' (What does Historical Learning Mean? A Definition in the Field of Tension Between Social Demands, Subjective Attributions of Meaning and Competences of Historical Thinking), in *Geschichtsunterricht im 21. Jahrhundert (History Classes in the 21th Century)*, eds. Thomas Sandkühler et al. (Göttingen, 2018), pp. 75–92.
22 Wolfgang Jacobmeyer, 'Konditionierung von Geschichtsbewusstsein. Schulbücher als nationale Autobiographien' (Conditioning of historical consciousness. Textbooks as national autobiographies), *Gruppendynamik* 23 (1992), pp. 375–388.
23 See Chapter 2.

6 Methodological suggestions and concrete tasks for working with this book at school and university level

Felix Hinz and Johannes Meyer-Hamme

Let us venture the following thesis: the text on the history of the Crusades presented here in an international comparison works well for a de-constructive, analytical examination. The central question is how the history of the Crusades is narrated in the selected historical cultures. Here, the question is not how students create historical meaning for themselves (based on their individual interpretations of the sources). The comparison-analytical approach presented here finds solid grounding in the dimensions of historical learning mentioned earlier.[1]

1 The comparison makes clear just how different the references and orientations are (e.g. territorially or politically), as well as to what extent the history of the Crusades is relevant today. Therefore, historical learning is not only an introduction to how the history of the Crusades is dealt with in societies, but also a reflection of the historical culture.
2 By de-constructing the narratives of the history of the Crusades – that is, the categories and concept which are employed – the skills of historical learning can be learned and reflected upon. At the same time, historical learning aims to elaborate the capacities and categories of historical thinking.
3 By analytically comparing how people (here: historians) today make connections to the history of the Crusades and orient themselves according to their present and future, the students face the challenge of how to relate to the different positions. Historical learning aims to give the participants the possibility to position themselves.

In order to apply the aforementioned texts on the history of the Crusades concretely, it is initially helpful to distinguish between the central questions for classes and concrete assignments. Both tasks should be problem-oriented and formulated openly. They should not be able to be answered with a simple, 'yes' or 'no'. Instead, they should require thorough assessment consideration and narration, e.g. arguments that lead to a historical judgement should be required. In order to cultivate a reflective handling of history through the examination of conflicting narratives, students should be given discussion assignments that cannot be clearly answered and are relevant in the sense of having a contemporary orientation function. One such approach is called problem-oriented. The problems that need to be worked on do not lie in the past, where they must only be found; rather, they arise more as a result of the question of orientation in regard to the future. Every problem-oriented leading question, every slightly dubious thesis that provokes contradiction or every contradiction that cannot be completely resolved, therefore, also has a reference to the present and the world, or points beyond the concrete historical object ('Crusades') by firstly training the categories and abilities of historical thinking, so that these can be applied to future historical orientation questions. At the same time, they serve as a reflection of historical cultures and make it possible to better judge one's own position and actively represent it. On the basis of the aforementioned material, with respect to the suggestions of Andreas Körber[2] on the arguments regarding orientations today, such problematized leading questions can also refer to the concrete narrations or environments of students. Questions on the history of the 'Crusades' can be formulated thus:

1 Contemporary Historical Orientations:

    1 To what extent do the interpretations of the history of the Crusades in the selected societies differ from each other today? – How are the differences explained and justified?
    2 To what extent are the histories of the Crusades addressed to specific groups? – To what extent are different groups construed by these histories? (e.g. ethnic, linguistic, religious or social groups).
    3 What role does the history of the Crusades play in the context of political, moral, religious, aesthetic and/or academic debates today? – Who advocates for which interpretations and why?
    4 …

2 Concrete Narratives in Comparison (as leading questions for individual lessons):

   1 How are the Crusades explained within different historical cultures?
   2 Which people and events of the past are mentioned or are central? Why these in particular? (e.g. Saladin? St. Henry? Kılıç Arslan? Or: the Battle of Didgori? the Battle of Hattin? the Battle of Grunwald/Tannenberg?)
   3 To what degree can the narratives be verified by sources – to what degree can they be described as myths? (e.g. Conquest of Damietta by William of Holland on the Third Crusade? The Danish flag falling from the sky at the Battle of Lyndanisse?)
   4 To what degree are the Crusades seen as a prelude to colonialism and imperialism? – How plausible are these positions?
   5 Some imply that the Crusades were wars of self-defence, while others suggest they were wars of aggression. Who suggests what and why?
   6 …

3 The Crusades in the Real-World Environment of Students:

   1 How do the students judge the Crusades as an argument for contemporary political and societal conflicts? – What are the ranges and limits of the arguments?
   2 To what extent is the media used by students (e.g. computer games) as a reference? How are groups construed therein ('us' or 'the others')?
   3 …

Each of these questions or subjects can only be answered with an 'on the one hand, yes, but on the other…'. This creates an awareness of the problems for students, which can be applied beyond history classes to many other areas of life in a globalized world, making this approach both didactically and pedagogically worthwhile.

Notes

1 See Chapter 5.

2 Andreas Körber, 'Die Kreuzzüge – ein ergiebiges Thema für (interkulturelles) historisches Lernen?' (The Crusades – A Profitable Subject for (Intercultural) Historical Learning?), in *Kreuzzüge des Mittelalters und der Neuzeit. Realhistorie – Geschichtskultur – Didaktik (Crusades of the Middle Ages and in the Modern Era. History – Historical Culture – Didactics)*, ed. Felix Hinz (Hildesheim, 2015), pp. 285–320.

7 Epilogue

Felix Hinz and Johannes Meyer-Hamme

The hope is that this book not only provides students with material illustrative of the controversies between historical cultures, but that it also offers suggestions for historians. As has been mentioned multiple times, that it cannot be claimed to have collected the entirety of perspectives, but at least brought attention to the range of interpretations. Interpretations that went beyond a qualitative content analysis and the assessment and evaluations of the individual contributions were held back. Corresponding valuations are left to the individual readers, as the contributions doubtlessly offer material for very different and fascinating discussions on many levels. It is highly doubtful that the opinions on this material will be unanimous.

However, the opinions do not have to be unanimous, since history was always a discursive subject. Furthermore, the *Debate on the Crusades* (Tyerman 2011) is as old as the phenomenon of the Crusades itself. So far, they have only been discussed in regard to historiographical research, but will continually be discussed as long as people believe that they will be able to attain orientation from the Crusades for their particular present and future. It is hoped that here a deeper exchange has been initiated.

From the view of the authors, three desiderata for further research and discussion emerge:

1 At the historiography level: a history of the Crusades from an interlinking historical perspective, one which integrates the different perspectives and narratives while, at the same time, disclosing the contradictions.
2 At the level of empirical research on historical consciousness in society: further studies on the contemporary understanding of the Crusades within different media sources and among different groups.

3 At the level of didactical research: concepts and their testing, that is, empirical studies, such as how adolescents deal with differing historical narratives about the history of the Crusades in a globalized world.

The need to deal with societal discourse that has contradictory historical narratives (not only the history of the Crusades) in politics and education shows up in the many historical cultures and historical–political discussions wherein this history is referenced.

Literature

Tyerman, Christopher, *The Debate on the Crusades* (Manchester, 2011).

Index

Note: **Bold** page numbers refer to tables; *italic* page numbers refer to figures and page numbers followed by "n" denote endnotes.

academic scholarship 121, 123
acquiring knowledge 11
Acre 2, 42, 45, 48, 62, 72, 108
aesthetic dimension 16, 113
Aleksejev, Tiit 89
Al-Hurub Al-Salibyya 45
Alphandéry, Paul 71; *La chrétienté et l'idée de croisade* 30
Anderson, Benedict 8
anti-religious project 27
anti-state terrorist organization 45
Arabic-speaking historical cultures 108
Aristeidou, Aikaterini 40
Arodaphnousa 41
Arup, Erik 51
Asbridge, Thomas 109
Ashby, Rosalyn 122, 126
al-Assad, Hafez 62
Aurell, Martin 30
Auto da Barca do Inferno (Vicente) 37
Avalishvili, Zurab 94

Ba'ath Party 62, 63
Balard, Michal: *Croisades et Orient latin* 30; *Latins en Orient XIe–XVe siècle* 30
Balfour Declaration 62
Baloup, Daniel 31
Baltic Crusades 64, 65, 89, 90, 114
Baltic States 3, 71, 105
Baptism 89
Beckman, Thea: *Kruistocht in spijkerbroek/Crusade in Jeans* 57, 112
Bibliothèque des croisades (Michaud) 29
Biget, Jean-Louis 31
bin Laden, Osama 16
Bjørnson, Bjørnstjerne 22
Bongars, Jacques: *Gesta Dei per Francos* 29
British historiography 117
Bulwark of Christianity 82
'Burgundian' period 57
Bush, George W. 2, 26, 78, 113, 116
Byzantine-Latin interaction 43
Byzantium 42, 47, 95

Carr, Edward H. 7
'Children's Crusade' 57, 76, 79, 109
Chladenius, Johann Martin 3
La chrétienté et l'idée de croisade (Alphandéry) 30
Christendom 1, 33, 34, 68, 70, 71
Christianity 27, 33, 65, 91, 116; Islam and 24–25, 88
Christianization 37, 89, 107
'clash of civilisations' 116
Clermont, Council of 36, 47
cognitive dimension 15, 110
Cohen, Jeffrey Jerome 8
colonialism 2, 11, 30, 62, 63, 71, 100
communism 54, 82

comparison-analytical approach 129
comprehensive historical culture 15
"concepts of the historians" 10–11
A Connecticut Yankee in King Arthur's Court (Twain) 78–79
'consensual objectivity' 15
Constantinople (today Istanbul)
'constructions of meaning' 12, **13**, 124
contemporary historical orientations 130
contemporary historiography of crusades 30
contemporary orientation function 130
conventional interpretations 125
Cowdrey, H.E.J. 67
Croisades et Orient latin (Balard) 30
Crusade in Europe (Eisenhower) 79
crusader movement 52, 95
Crusades: deplorable 64–66; historical narratives on 7; historiography of 117; and maritime expansion 36–37; public interest in 2; as *Reconquista* 53–55; state of continuous rape and violation 62–63
The Crusades (DeMille) 79
Cypriot agricultural products 40

Danish identity 51
Danto, Arthur C. 7–9, 12, 124
Debate on the Crusades (Tyerman) 132
De croisade (Dupront) 30
DeMille, Cecil B.: *The Crusades* 79
Deschamps, Paul 31
Dias, Dinis 36
digital communication tools 5
Doctrine of Pope Gelasius 71
dominant historical narratives 8
dominant interpretative schema 43
Dupront, Alphonse 71; *De croisade* 30

Egypt, crusades in 45–46
Egyptian educational system 45
'Ehl-i Salîb' 47
Eighth Army's Operation Crusader 60
Eisenhower, Dwight D.: *Crusade in Europe* 79
Enlightenment 16, 59, 89, 118n8
Erdmann, Carl 67; *The Origins of the Idea of Crusading* 84
Estonia: crusades in 89–90; historical culture 106–107
Estonian historical scholarship 90
Estonian national identity 90
European historical cultures 3
Europeanization of Finland 65
Evans, Richard 14; *In Defence of History* 12

Fatimid dynasty 45
Fifth Crusade 75
Finland, crusades in 65, 91–93
Finnish historical culture 106–108
'Finnish identity' 92
Finnish Lutheran 92
First Crusade 1, 15, 33, 45, 48, 50, 56–57, 63, 68, 71, 73, 75, 87, 91–92, 94, 108; to Finland 65
Fletcher, Roger 53
Flori, Jean 57
form of a presentation 11
Fourth Crusade 42, 43, 117n4
France, crusades in 29–31, 70–71
'Frankish invasions' 24–25
French Roman Catholic dynasty 39
Friedman, Yvonne 72
function of orientation 11

George, Lloyd 59
Georgian historiography 94, 95
German civilisation 81
Gerusalemme Liberata (Tasso) 87
Gesta Dei per Francos (Bongars) 29
Gibbon, Edward 59
Gouraud, Henri 62
Greco-Latin interaction 42–44
Greek Church of Cyprus 39
Greek Cypriot 39–41; culture 41; historiography 40
Greek dialect of Cyprus 40
Grieg, Edvard 22
Grousset, René 29
Guiscard, Robert 33
Guiscard, Roger 33

Haakon IV Haakonson (King of Norway) 21
Hagenmeyer, Heinrich 84

Haskins, Charles Homer: *The Renaissance of the Twelfth Century* 79
'Hellenism under Foreign Domination' 43
Higounet, Charles: *Les Allemands en Europe centrale et orientale au Moyen Age* 31
Histoire de Belgique (Pirenne) 56
Histoire des croisades (Richard and Michaud) 29, 30
historical competencies 124
historical culture 2–5, 7, 12, 14–15, 17, 98, 100, 105, 106, 110–117, 119, 121, 125, 126, 130; aesthetic dimension 16; Arabic-speaking 108; cognitive dimension 15; "concepts of the historians" 10–11; 'constructions of meaning' 12, **13**; dominant historical narratives 8; of Estonia 106–107; of Europe 3; of Finland 107; historical narrations 10; historical thinking 9; of Syria 108
historical education 17, 109; academic scholarship 121, 123; didactical conclusions 121; Estonian historical scholarship 90; historical learning 119, 120; Seixas, Peter 120–122
historical knowledge 12
historical learning 14, 18, 119, 120, 122–127, 129
historical narrations 3, 8–11, 14, 122, 124–126
historical narratives 3, 7–9, 11, 99, 122, 125–127, 133
historical thinking 9, *10,* 11, 12, 15, 17, 19n24, 117, 117n2, 121, 124, 126, 127; categories and abilities to 130; competence model of 124, 125; structural characteristics of 12; structural model of 7
A History of the Crusades (Runciman) 60, 110
Hume, David 59
Huntington, Samuel P. 26

Iberian Christian ideology 53
'identity machine' 8
imagined communities 8
In Defence of History (Evans) 12
indulgences 37, 89
intellectual discourse 73
interwar organization 60
'invented traditions' 99
Islam: Byzantium and 39; and Christianity 24–25; inherent violent religion of 115; political and aggressive form of 2; and Tibetan Buddhism 27; warfare against 53
'Islamic Crusade' 86
Islamic culture 27
Islamic terrorism 54, 115
'Island of the Knights' 33–34
Israeli collective memory 73, 74
Israeli intellectual discourse 73
Italian historiographic tradition 87

Jenkins, Keith 7, 12
Jerusalem
Jewish community 1
Jewish religious education 1
Jews 1, 72, 73
João II (King John II, King of Portugal) 37

Kelly, Axel 67
Kilij Arslan I (Sultan of the Seljuks of Rûm) 47, 48
knowledge: acquiring 11; historical 12
König, Joel 2, 3
Körber, Andreas 9, 124, 130
Kruistocht in spijkerbroek/Crusade in Jeans (Beckman) 57, 112

Latins en Orient XIe–XVe siècle (Balard) 30
Lavigerie, Charles Martial Allemand 29
Lea, Henry Charles 78
Lee, Peter 122, 126
Legenda sancti Henrici 92
Les Allemands en Europe centrale et orientale au Moyen Age (Higounets) 31
Levantine Crusades 82
Lusignan (French dynasty) 39

Magnus Eriksson (King of Sweden and Norway) 64
Maltese historical culture 100

'manifest destiny' 25, 79
Manifestus probatum est 36
Manuel, King D. 37
Marxist approach 23
Marxist historiography 90, 112
Mayer, Hans Eberhard 84
McCann, Conor 67
Medieval Crusades 56, 60, 65–67, 80, 91, 115
medieval Islamic historiography 24
Merkel, Garlieb 89
Mesud I (Sultan of the Seljuks of Rûm) 48
Metsanurk, Mait: *Ümera jõel* 89
Meyer-Hamme, Johannes 126
Michaud, Joseph: *Bibliothèque des croisades* 29; *Histoire des croisades* 29
Mickiewicz, Adam 82
modern historiography 65
Moorish Iberian Peninsula 105
moral dimension 16, 114
'Muistne vabadusvõitlus' 89
Munthe, Gerhard 22
Murray, Alan V. 57
Muslim communities 33
'Muslim factor' 27
Muslim fundamentalist 45

'narrative-families' 106
'national autobiographies' 126
National Socialism 1
national-socialist ideology 99
Nazism 54
neo-colonial doctrines 25
'neo-Crusades' 25, 26
Ní Chléirigh, Léan 67
Norwegian Crusading 21–23
Norwegian historiography 22, 23
Nur ad-Din Zengi 48

O'Callaghan, Joseph F. 53
O'Hanrahan, Michael: *When the Norman Came* 68
Order of Christ 36
'Ordines Militares' conference 81, 85
The Origins of the Idea of Crusading (Erdmann) 84
Ormson, Erling 21
Orthodox Christianity 106
Ottoman Conquest 40
Ottoman Siege 33–34

Palestine, crusades in 45–46
Papadopoullos, Theodore 39
Paparrigopoulos, Konstantinos 43
Paschal II (Latin Pope) 36
Paul, Nicholas 57
Paviot, Jacques 31
Pegg, Mark 113, 116
'Period of the Crusades' 31, 39, 65, 91
Phillips, Jonathan 57
Piispa Henrikin surmavirsi 92
Pirenne, Henri: *Histoire de Belgique* 56
pluralistic approach 90
Poland, crusades in 81–82
Polish communist regime 81
Polish-Lithuanian Commonwealth 82
political dimension 16, 113, 114, 116
Prawer, Joshua 72

Reagan, Ronald 26
Reconquista 53–55
Recueil des Historiens des Croisades (Riant) 29, 70
'regional narrative families' 100
religious dimension 16, 24, 79, 110, 115, 116
religious diversity 27
religious extremism 27
religious justification 64
religious war 26, 27, 94
The Renaissance of the Twelfth Century (Haskins) 79
Riant, Paul 22, 51; *Recueil des Historiens des Croisades* 29, 70; *Société de l'Orient latin* 29
Richard, Jean: *Histoire des croisades* 30
Richard the Lionheart (Richard I, King of England) 59–61
Riley-Smith, Jonathan 60, 67
Ristikivi, Karl 89
ristiretki 91
Robinson, Ian Stuart 67
Röhricht, Reinhold 84
Romanticism 78
Runciman, Sir Steven: *A History of the Crusades* 60, 110

Rüsen, Jörn 8, 9, 14, 15, 17, 106, 124
Russian civilization 27

Scandinavian historiography 64
scholarship: academic 121, 123; Estonian historical 90
Schreiber, Waltraud 124
scientific community 4
Scott, Walter 59, 78; *The Talisman* 16, 112
Second Crusade 36, 50, 51, 65, 82, 91
second-order concepts 122–124
secularism 26
Seixas, Peter 120–123, 126, 127
Sigurd I Magnusson (King of Norway) 21–23
Skottki, Kristin 8, 15
socially conventional interpretations 14
Société de l'Orient latin (Riant) 29
Spain, crusades in 53–55
Steenstrup, Johannes 51
Steen, Thorvald 23
structuralism 70–71
surmavirsi 92
Swedish Crusades 64, 91, 106
Swedish–Finnish realm 65
Swedish historiography 65
Syria, crusades in 62–63

The Talisman (Scott) 16, 112
Tasso, Torquato: *Gerusalemme Liberata* 87
Teutonic Order 64, 65, 81, 82, 84–86, 113
Third Crusade 21, 39, 40, 65, 75, 76, 82, 91, 108, 110
Traditional Spanish historiography 53
Treaty of Sèvres 48
Treitschke, Heinrich von 85
Trump, Donald 78, 116
Turkey, crusades in 47–48
Twain, Mark: *A Connecticut Yankee in King Arthur's Court* 78–79

Ümera jõel (Metsanurk) 89
Urban II (Pope)

Vicente, Gil: *Auto da Barca do Inferno* 37

Wendish Crusade 50
Western colonialism 62, 63
Western European colonialism 42
Western feudal system 39
When the Norman Came (O'Hanrahan) 68
Wineburg, Sam 123–124

Zakkar, Soheil 62
Zengi, Imad ad-Din (Oghuz-Turkey atabeg) 48
Zerner, Monique 31
Zionism 62, 63
Zionist movement 73

For Product Safety Concerns and Information please contact our EU representative GPSR@taylorandfrancis.com
Taylor & Francis Verlag GmbH, Kaufingerstraße 24, 80331 München, Germany

www.ingramcontent.com/pod-product-compliance
Lightning Source LLC
LaVergne TN
LVHW020628100826
845148LV00012B/2092
* 9 7 8 0 3 6 7 5 1 1 2 7 2 *